HEALING BALM FOR THE SOUL

Michael Nwaduba

Grosvenor House
Publishing Limited

This book is published by
Grosvenor House Publishing Ltd
Link House
140 The Broadway, Tolworth, Surrey, KT6 7HT.
www.grosvenorhousepublishing.co.uk

NOTE:
The information and views expressed in this book by the author should not be used as a substitute for professional medical advice or treatment, always consult your doctor. Any use of the information in this book is entirely at the reader's discretion and risk. The author or publisher cannot be held liable for any loss, claim, or damages arising out of the use or misuse of the suggestions made in this book.

Due to the dynamic nature of the internet, website addresses or links used in this book may have changed since publication and may no longer be valid. Hence, the author and publisher hereby disclaim any responsibility for them.

A CIP record for this book
is available from the British Library

ISBN 978-1-78623-469-8

CONTENTS

ABOUT THE BOOK HEALING BALM FOR THE SOUL

I published my first book entitled – ***A Simple Guide for Bible Study*** in 2008. This was followed by my second book, ***Questions and Answers on Tithes: Covenant of Prosperity*** which was published in 2009. After the publication of this book, I tried and tried to write another book but I couldn't. Every time inspiration to write came, it always ended up in an article. It never translated into a book. So I ended up writing many articles through the inspiration of the Holy Spirit. I wrote over three hundred articles from between 2009 and 2017.

Healing Balm for the Soul is a compilation of selected articles I wrote between 2009 and 2017 when I finally got the inspiration to write the book – ***Amazing Grace in Abundance***.

It didn't make any sense to me that I should just write articles and keep them, so I featured many of the articles you will find in this book on my Facebook and WhatsApp accounts so that somebody can read them and be blessed. Hence, most of the articles you will find in this book have been featured on social media. If you come across any of these articles in this book just know I am the author.

The articles you will read in this book are all independent, which means you can read them at random as you choose to. Yet a combination of all of them will bring forth holistic healing – wholesomeness! Receive your healing by faith as you read this book in Jesus' name. Amen!

MICHAEL NWADUBA

CHAPTER ONE

HE RESTORES MY SOUL – PSALM 23:3

Some years ago, I went through some challenges that shattered me emotionally. It seemed like my whole world was turned upside down. The very foundation of my being was indeed struck hard emotionally and needed to be restored. At this point, the Holy Spirit led me to reach out for my Bible which I started devouring voraciously. The Psalmist declared ***in Psalm 119:71***, *"It is good for me that I have been afflicted: that I might learn thy statutes."* Affliction time is time to learn the Word of God.

In my desperate bid to be healed emotionally, I was led to get out my concordance and compile healing scriptures that I focused on, read, and confessed regularly.

HEALING SCRIPTURES

Isaiah 53:5

> *But he was wounded for our transgressions, he was bruised for our iniquities: the chastisement of our peace was upon him; and with his stripes we are healed.*

Jeremiah 17:14

> *Heal me, O LORD, and I shall be healed; save me, and I shall be saved: for thou art my praise.*

Psalm 147:3

> *He healeth the broken in heart, and bindeth up their wounds.*

Jeremiah 30:17

For I will restore health unto thee, and I will heal thee of thy wounds, saith the LORD; because they called thee an outcast, saying, this is Zion, whom no man seeketh after.

Matthew 4:23

And Jesus went about all Galilee, teaching in their synagogues, and preaching the gospel of the kingdom, and healing all manner of sickness and all manner of disease among the people.

Exodus 15:26

And said, If thou wilt diligently hearken to the voice of the LORD thy God, and wilt do that which is right in his sight, and wilt give *ear to his commandments, and keep all his statutes, I will put none of these diseases upon thee, which I have brought upon the Egyptians: for I am the LORD that healeth thee.*

Psalm 107:20

He sent his word, and healed them, *and delivered them from their destructions.*

Jeremiah 8:21–22

21 *For the hurt of the daughter of my people am I hurt; I am black; astonishment hath taken hold on me.*

22 *Is there no balm in Gilead; is there no physician there? why then is not the health of the daughter of my people recovered?*

1 Peter 2:24

Who his own self bare our sins in his own body on the tree, that we, being dead to sins, should live unto righteousness: by whose stripes ye were healed.

Mark 6:13

And they cast out many devils, and anointed with oil many that were sick, and healed them.

Acts 19:11–12

[11]*And God wrought special miracles by the hands of Paul:*

[12] *So that from his body were brought unto the sick handkerchiefs or aprons, and the diseases departed from them, and the evil spirits went out of them.*

Isaiah 10:27

And it shall come to pass in that day, that his burden shall be taken away from off thy shoulder, and his yoke from off thy neck, and the yoke shall be destroyed because of the anointing.

Isaiah 33:24

And the inhabitant shall not say, I am sick: the people that dwell therein shall be forgiven their iniquity.

Joel 3:10

Beat your ploughshares into swords, and your pruning hooks into spears: let the weak say, I am strong.

3 John 1:2

Beloved, I wish above all things that thou mayest prosper and be in health, even as thy soul prospereth.

Psalm 107:2

Let the redeemed of the LORD say so, whom he hath redeemed from the hand of the enemy;

John 8:36

If the Son therefore shall make you free, ye shall be free indeed.

My focus was on reading, meditating, and praying with the above scriptures, as well as studying most of other parts of the Bible, and as I did this, my soul was restored back, without me even realising it and how. God worked on me internally and perfected that which concerned my spirit, soul, and body. Hallelujah!

God created human beings, and as our creator, He provided us with a life manual called the Holy Bible or the Word of God which we can use to fix our health, finances, relationships, family, career, and other areas of our life.

Looking at the above healing scriptures, God specifically said in ***Jeremiah 30:17***, "*For I will restore health unto thee, and I will heal thee of thy wounds, saith the* L*ORD; because they called thee an outcast, saying, This is Zion, whom no man seeketh after.*" God has promised here that He will restore health and heal His people of their wounds. It's important that we hold on faithfully to these words until we see it manifest.

And Jesus said in ***John 6:63***, "*It is the spirit that quickeneth; the flesh profiteth nothing: the words that I speak unto you, they are spirit, and they are life.*" Jesus states here that the words that He declares give life. He is talking about the Word of God.

Proverbs 4:20-22 also says,

> 20*My son, attend to my words; incline thine ear unto my sayings.*
>
> 21*Let them not depart from thine eyes; keep them in the midst of thine heart.*
>
> 22*For they are life unto those that find them, and health to all their flesh.*

God is faithful. Whatever He says in His Word, He is forever committed to do. He is not man that He should lie. The Word of God is life and health to the flesh. I have seen and heard testimonies of people who held on to the Word of God and received their healing. Hold on to His Word and He will restore your soul. ***Psalm 23:3*** says, "*He restoreth my soul: he leadeth me in the paths of righteousness for his name's sake.*"

CHAPTER TWO

THERE IS TIME FOR EVERYTHING – ECCLESIASTES 3:1

The Bible makes it clear in the Book of ***Ecclesiastes 3:1*** that, "*To everything there is a season, and a time to every purpose under the heaven:*"

As ambitious, hardworking, and perhaps desperate we may be, our desired goals may not materialise if it's not yet God's appointed time. If you like cry, shed tears, or even threaten God, there are certain things that will only happen at a given time as defined by God in the events of life. God made it like that so that there will be order. He says in ***1 Corinthians 14:40***, "*Let all things be done decently and in order.*"

The interesting thing about God's timing is that His timing is perfect. He does not come too early or too late. Read further down from Ecclesiastes 3:1–8 and see that the Bible states clearly that there is time for a number of different things.

The Psalmist says in ***Psalm 102:13***, "*Thou shalt arise, and have mercy upon Zion: for the time to favour her, yea, the set time, is come.*" There is a set time for God's favour to manifest. You can't force it. There is certainly a set time for everything and trying to hurry up things may lead to premature manifestation, and this could lead to a disaster. Patience is therefore a necessary virtue required for the full manifestations of God's promises in our life. We are all in this life to run our individual races. Do not be distracted by others who are running their own race. Therefore, remain on your track, and keep looking unto Jesus, the author and finisher of our faith.

Interestingly, apart from God, men have also set time for different things in life. For example, there is a set time and age for nursery, primary, secondary, and university education for a child's proper development. No matter how smart a seven-year-old child may be, he is not meant to drive until he is seventeen years old. Timing!

Isaiah 46:10,*"Declaring the end from the beginning, and from ancient times the things that are not yet done, saying, My counsel shall stand, and I will do all my pleasure:"* Revelation 1:8 tells us that Jesus is Alpha and Omega, the beginning and the end of all things. Before He formed you in your mother's womb, He knew you and predestined what you will be, and nothing can change His counsel. It will all come to pass at His appointed time.

Sometimes we are in a hurry to see certain things happen. And because of this, some people cut corners or scheme to see things happen fast. They think God is too slow therefore they want to help Him to speed up things.

There is this woman called Janet who was in her late thirties, and was in a hurry to start a family because all her friends are married with children. She was fortunate to meet a man who also liked her, but she hastily moved in to live with the man even before proper courtship and wedding, and in no time she was pregnant and the relationship hit the rocks and collapsed. Afterwards, she regretted being in too much haste because that did not allow for a proper foundation to be laid. And if the foundation be destroyed, what can the righteous do? Delay is not denial. If we want to be honest to ourselves, there are things that seemed to have been delayed before we received them, and we will thank God for delaying it because if it had arrived earlier, we would have misused it due to lack of experience and maturity.

Some years ago, I took my friend's five-year-old son out to play in the park, and he requested freshly fried cod fish and chips and after it was served I said, "Patrick leave it to cool down a bit before you start eating," he got upset, started crying, and fell down on the floor in protest that he wants it now. To appease him and also let him learn a lesson that hot food hurts, I let him have his hot cod fish and chips. Immediately he grabbed the cod fish, he dropped it back on the plate and said, "Uncle Mike, it's too hot."

And I said, "I told you that but you won't listen to me."

He had to experience for himself that hot food can hurt, and he had to now wait patiently for the food to cool down before eating and enjoyed it. That's exactly how some of us present our requests to God impatiently, and if it turns up too early, we misuse it because it is too hot for us. And we are too immature to handle it. ***Ecclesiastes 3:11***, says, "*He hath made everything beautiful in his time: also he hath set the world in their heart, so that no man can find out the work that God maketh from the beginning to the end.*" Be patient and let God make all things beautiful at His own appointed time and not yours.

CHAPTER THREE

DO NOT WORRY – MATTHEW 6:25 NIV

WORRY VERSUS MEDITATION

WORRY is unnecessary negative pondering or dwelling on issues that a person should let go. It is bad and unhealthy and can actually become a stronghold if the person continues to constantly dwell on such negative, unproductive, fearful things which may not happen after all.

THE DISADVANTAGES OF WORRY

Worry has no benefits. This goes to show how terrible worry is. I have discussed below some of these terrible disadvantages so that we can effectively get rid of all worries.

1. It makes the person lose their peace.
2. Worrying does not change or improve the situation of things, instead it worsens it.
3. Worry produces fear, instead of faith.
4. Worry is proof of a lack of trust in God to help you.
5. Worry exposes people to satanic attack.
6. Worry is unhealthy and can lead to emotional sicknesses like stress and depression.
7. Worry weakens the power of God within a person.
8. The more a person worries about something, the more that problem is likely to be enlarged like a balloon until it becomes a stronghold.

Read below Jesus' advice on worry.

Matthew 6:25-28

> [25]*Therefore I say unto you, Take no thought for your life, what ye shall eat, or what ye shall drink; nor yet for your body, what ye shall put on. Is not the life more than meat, and the body than raiment?*
>
> [26]*Behold the fowls of the air: for they sow not, neither do they reap, nor gather into barns; yet your heavenly Father feedeth them. Are ye not much better than they?*
>
> [27]*Which of you by taking thought can add one cubit unto his stature?*
>
> [28]*And why take ye thought for raiment? Consider the lilies of the field, how they grow; they toil not, neither do they spin.*

MEDITATION on the other hand is about dwelling on the scriptures and this produces faith to empower us. When you meditate on the Word of God, you compare scriptures with scriptures, and analyse verses as you yield and cooperate with the Holy Spirit. The Psalmist says in ***Psalms 119:99***, *"I have more understanding than all my teachers: for thy testimonies are my meditation."*

Meditation focuses on positive things and will also bring about the solution to the challenge, but worry will simply worsen the situation. It's important to mention here that if you know how to worry, it's an indication that you will also know how to meditate. All you have to do is switch from dwelling on negative unproductive issues, and focus on pondering on the Word of God, and positive issues.

The Bible says that Isaac went to the field, and as he meditated, his bride Rebekah manifested *in* ***Genesis 24:63–64*** that says,

> [63]*And Isaac went out to meditate in the field at the eventide: and he lifted up his eyes, and saw, and, behold, the camels were coming.*
>
> [64]*And Rebekah lifted up her eyes, and when she saw Isaac, she lighted off the camel.*

Stop worrying and start meditating on the Word of God and see the power of God in operation and the solution to that which you desire. ***Philippians 4:8*** tells us what to meditate on as Christians. It says, "*Finally, brethren, whatsoever things are true, whatsoever things are honest, whatsoever things are just, whatsoever things are pure, whatsoever things are lovely, whatsoever things are of good report; if there be any virtue, and if there be any praise, think on these things.*"

CHAPTER FOUR

THE GREAT EARTHQUAKE – ACTS 16:26

When you hear of a great earthquake, the first thing that comes to mind is, "O my God, a lot of people must have died." But the good news about this great earthquake is that when it struck, Paul and Silas who were in bondage in prison had their chains loosed, and the prison doors opened. They were supernaturally freed. Nobody died. Yet, it was a great earthquake. Hallelujah!

Act 16:23–26

> 23*And when they had laid many stripes upon them, they cast them into prison, charging the jailor to keep them safely:*
>
> 24*Who, having received such a charge, thrust them into the inner prison, and made their feet fast in the stocks.*
>
> 25*And at midnight Paul and Silas prayed, and sang praises unto God: and the prisoners heard them.*
>
> 26*And suddenly there was a great earthquake, so that the foundations of the prison were shaken: and immediately all the doors were opened, and everyone's bands were loosed.*

What an earthquake! I call it the earthquake of freedom. This earthquake was triggered by the tremendous power of prayer and praises by two Men of God. Awesome! Some years ago, I went into serious praise and worship onto the Lord to the extent that there was a shaking similar to the earthquake described here. I was supernaturally loosed and set free from the trials I was facing then, and the Lord opened new doors of favour for me, and even gave me a new song. Awesome! Apart from my own personal praise experience, I have also heard testimonies of people who got into serious prayers and praises, and they were delivered from their bondage, and gained victory over the works of the devil. An example from the Bible tells us that the only thing king Jehoshaphat and the people of Judah did in order to triumph over their enemies, was to praise God in ***2 Chronicles 20:22*** that says, *"And when they began to sing and praise, the LORD set ambushments against the children of Ammon, Moab, and mount Seir, which were come against Judah, and they were smitten."*

My prayer today is that there shall be a sudden divine great earthquake that will strike and go down to the foundations of challenges to uproot, and destroy them permanently in Jesus' name. Every chain, bondage, and yoke of affliction shall be loosed and destroyed all to the glory of God as you pray and praise Him. I declare total freedom in Jesus' name. ***John 8:36*** says, *"If the Son therefore, shall make you free, ye shall be free indeed."*

CHAPTER FIVE

JUST SAY SORRY

Genuinely saying sorry happens to be the hardest thing to do for some people, but it shouldn't really be so. It's a true demonstration of the character of God that a person transgresses whether against God or a fellow man and says sorry, and means it. This automatically helps to enable you have a free mind as well as be at peace with whoever you need to apologise to. The peace of God that surpasses all understanding is even more precious than gold. When you are at peace with yourself and fellow men, it opens unexplainable doors of progress and prosperity. And mind you, when you say sorry to a person, it does not necessarily mean you are wrong. It simply means you want to be at peace with the person, and it is indeed the right thing to do. People have wronged me several times, and I still humbled myself for the sake of peace and say sorry to them.

THINGS TO KNOW ABOUT SAYING SORRY

1. Peace will reign. See Matthew 5:9 – This makes you a true child of God.
2. You will avoid further argument.
3. You will help your spiritual life to remain strong by not allowing strife.
4. When you genuinely say sorry and the person you said sorry to will not accept your apology, leave them alone and move on with your life.
5. Remember, your sorry may not be accepted if your tone does not convey genuine remorse and repentance. Therefore, say sorry and mean it.

6. Say sorry at the right time. Don't say sorry next month when you can say it now or today. When sorry is not said at the right time, it may be meaningless.
7. Note that it is better to do the right thing and avoid saying sorry. Your sorry may not be accepted if you are known to say sorry after doing the wrong thing deliberately.
8. Proud and wicked people don't say sorry. They hurt people and are not bothered. It's better not to join them.
9. To say sorry to people you offend is about sowing a good seed. People will also say sorry to you when they hurt you.
10. Try not to demand sorry or apologies from people who hurt you. You will not fully enjoy the pleasure of their apology when you demand it. Sorry should flow naturally from the heart of the person saying it in order for it to be meaningful.
11. Sorry can act as a healing balm to those you hurt, or those who are in pain. So say it.
12. Saying sorry can save your marriage and other relationships. So say it and save your relationship.
13. Remember, to say sorry will not reduce your dignity, instead it will increase it.
14. Take advantage of this message and say sorry to someone who deserves it.

One last point that needs to be discussed here is the fact that when some people are offended, they expect the offender to say sorry before they will forgive them. It shouldn't really be so. Forgive everyone who offends you even if they don't say sorry. It is for your own good that you forgive, and avoid carrying the weight of grudges about. Remember, we live in a world where some people blindly claim to be right even when they are wrong, and this sadly sometimes includes us.

CHAPTER SIX

COMFORT OTHERS – 2 CORINTHIANS 1:3–4

The Most High God is indeed a comforter. When Jesus exited the earth, God sent us the Holy Spirit also known as the comforter to comfort us at all times. We are also expected to comfort our fellow brethren using the comfort and experience we have gained from the trials we've been through. The brokenness, sufferings, and chastisements we went through during trials were allowed by God, so that we can use them to comfort our fellow brethren. Therefore, we should not be ashamed to share our weaknesses, disappointments, and failures because they are valuable as we begin to use the experiences to comfort others. That's when pain is turned to gain.

There are people whose ministry are born out of the pain and trials they've been through. For example, we have activists, and campaigners who fight against oppressions, and their fight for human rights and freedom for people is as a result of what they've been through. They fight against injustice because they have been through it. The cracks, damages, and brokenness we've been through in life are meant to make us more beautiful and better people. Use what you have been through to inspire and comfort somebody else.

I once met a black African Solicitor in London and we got talking about immigration issues in Britain. He now told me he went through many years of hell before his immigration status was regularised for him to be granted indefinite leave to remain in the United Kingdom by the Home Office. He said he vowed afterwards that he will do whatever he could to help people in the area of immigration. Straightaway, he went to the University and studied for LLB (Hons) Law and proceeded to become a solicitor. In his zeal to achieve his goal of comforting people facing immigration challenges, he initially started by helping his clients absolutely free of charge, and he did that with huge success. It was when he started growing so much that he started charging money. That's an example of somebody comforting others as a result of the pain they have been through.

I met Margaret Mpofu, a South African, in London some years ago at a convention and we got talking. I asked her what she does for a living. She wholeheartedly gave me her life history, full of brokenness without being ashamed at all. She told me she runs an Orphanage home in South Africa. She was raised in an Orphanage in South Africa, and she didn't know who her parents were up to when we met. She said she's been through tough times and pain in life as an orphan, and as a result she vowed to fight until her last breath to help orphans. At the time I met her, she was doing absolutely fine fulfilling her dream to help orphans. This is another example of a person comforting others as a result of the pain they've been through in life.

2 Corinthians 1:3–4

> 3 *Blessed be God, even the Father of our Lord Jesus Christ, the Father of mercies, and the God of all comfort;*
>
> 4 *Who comforteth us in all our tribulation, that we may be able to comfort them which are in any trouble, by the comfort wherewith we ourselves are comforted of God.*

One of the easiest ways to rise to the top is to help people. Zig Ziglar said, "You can have whatever you want if you simply help enough people get what they want." Whao! That's a wisdom nugget for you. To get what you want in life, be ready to make it happen for others, and then it will come to you with ease. This means you have to love people, serve and help people, sacrifice, commit, and invest in people avoiding selfishness.

Jesus also gave His disciples this same powerful secret for greatness when he told them that the only way to be the chief disciple is to be servant to all. Read what He said in ***Matthew 20:26-28***

> [26]*But it shall not be so among you: but whosoever will be great among you, let him be your minister;*
>
> [27]*And whosoever will be chief among you, let him be your servant:*
>
> [28]*Even as the Son of man came not to be ministered unto, but to minister, and to give his life a ransom for many.*

My prayer is that the Lord shall turn every pain and challenge we go through in life into perpetual gain. The pain will translate into a formidable well established glorious ministry to help and comfort others in Jesus' name. Amen!

CHAPTER SEVEN

LET THIS MIND BE IN YOU – PHILIPPIANS 2:5

Let this mind be in you, which was also in Christ Jesus is simply saying let your way of thinking be godly and based on the Word of God as the main software running engine. Some people think the mind is the same as the heart organ that pumps blood along the arteries and veins to various parts of the body, or the brain that is linked to the spinal cord and the nervous system that processes information, but it's not. The mind is intangible, and therefore cannot be touched, or seen with the physical eyes, yet it exists as part of the soul linking the spirit. The soul is made up of three essential parts as follows – mind, emotion, and will (MEW). Therefore, the mind resides in the soul but you cannot touch or see it with your eyes.

When a computer software application is corrupted, what you do is download the corrupted software application and upload a new one. Similarly, some people are running their lives with corrupted worldly software minds that need to be downloaded, and to upload the Word of God into their mind to enable them function properly. The Bible says in ***Philippians 2:5***, *"Let this mind be in you, which was also in Christ Jesus:"* The mind of Christ is a renewed mind, saturated with the Word of God as the main running software engine. This software engine is pure, and as silver, it has been tried in the furnace of the earth purified seven times according to the Psalmist.

The book of ***Romans 8:6*** tells us that, *"For to be carnally minded is death; but to be spiritually minded is life and peace."* This is simply a summary of what should be expected to happen when the mind is corrupted, and it is not being run with the right software – The Word of God. Even a computer is likely to crash and pack up if the memory is corrupted or if it is being run with the wrong software.

The Bible says again in ***Romans 12:2,*** *"And be not conformed to this world: but be ye transformed by the renewing of your mind, that ye may prove what is that good, and acceptable, and perfect, will of God."* This scripture is urging us not to be conformed to this world with worldly ideas and mentality, but to renew our minds with the Word of God which has the ability of transforming our lives.

Saturating the mind with scriptures gives it a solid base for meditation. And this helps the spirit, soul, and body to function more efficiently. The human mind functions very much like a computer memory because it is the main engine. And as the computer jargon goes, 'garbage in garbage out.' Whatever you feed the computer is what it will process and give as output based on the input. Similarly, whatever we feed the mind is what it will process and give an output based on input. That's why it's important to have a renewed mind rather than a corrupt mind. King Solomon says in ***Proverbs 23:7***, *"For as he thinketh in his heart, so is he: Eat and drink, saith he to thee; but his heart is not with thee."* The heart this scripture is talking about is not actually the human heart that pumps blood, but the mind situated in the soul. This scripture can actually be paraphrased to be, "For as he thinketh in his ***mind***, so is he:..." Whatever we manifest in our life is a product of our thoughts. For example, what you type into a computer word processor is what will be printed out. Therefore, it's important to meditate on the Word of God, and dwell on positive things in our mind.

Just to mention a few benefits of having a renewed mind, note that a renewed mind thinks, speaks, and acts positively. A renewed mind sees things from a biblical point of view. It also makes the Word of God the ultimate standard for life application. A renewed mind does not worry, and it hardly falls sick because the renewed spirit of a man also sustains the body. Prophet Jeremiah was so excited about the Word of God to the extent that he says in ***Jeremiah 15:16***, "*Thy words were found, and I did eat them; and thy word was unto me the joy and rejoicing of mine heart: for I am called by thy name, O Lord God of hosts.*" Eat the Word of God, and meditate on it, to energise yourself.

CHAPTER EIGHT

THE HOLY SPIRIT – JOHN 14:26

John 14:26 (Amplified)

> *"But the Comforter (Counsellor, Helper, Intercessor, Advocate, Strengthener, Standby), the Holy Spirit, Whom the Father will send in My name [in My place, to represent Me and act on My behalf], He will teach you all things. And He will cause you to recall (will remind you of, bring to your remembrance) everything I have told you."*

John 14:26 of the Amplified Bible tells us that the Holy Spirit is our:

1. Comforter
2. Counsellor
3. Helper
4. Intercessor
5. Advocate
6. Strengthener
7. Standby
8. Teacher
9. Reminder

Whao! I'm excited to know the Holy Spirit will do all the above for me. As a Christian, you are born again, with recreated spirit, and the Holy Spirit dwells within you. 1 John 4:4 says He (The Holy Spirit) that is in you, is greater than he (The devil) that's in the world.

As a Christian, who do you go to first when you need comfort, counsel, help, intercession, legal support, strength, standby, teaching, or a reminder? Do you first go to men and things or to the Holy Spirit? Henceforth, ensure you go to the Holy Spirit first, because He is the spirit of truth. I have been in certain circumstances beyond me and all I simply did was to cry out to the Holy Spirit to help me because He is my Helper. For example, even in things one may consider as little, I have had to ask the Holy Spirit to help me. When I searched for my bunch of keys one day and I couldn't find it, I simply asked the Holy Spirit to reveal where the keys are, and He showed it to me.

John 16:13

> *"Howbeit when he, the Spirit of truth, is come, he will guide you into all truth: for he shall not speak of himself; but whatsoever he shall hear, that shall he speak: and he will shew you things to come."*

When you depend on the Holy Spirit, He will manifest Himself to you more. The Holy Spirit is a gentle spirit. As Christians, it is our duty to create the right atmosphere and situations that will welcome the full manifestation of the power of the Holy Spirit. The Holy Spirit is a person and that's why 'He' is used for Him and not 'It.' Therefore, don't grieve the Holy Spirit. The Holy Spirit can be grieved. ***Ephesians 4:30*** says, *"And grieve not the Holy Spirit of God, whereby ye are sealed unto the day of redemption."* The Holy Spirit is part of the Godhead or Trinity. Hence, He has similar characteristics, and capacity as God, and Jesus. So, rely on Him to live your life. He is the Comforter God sent to be with us after Jesus exit the earth.

CHAPTER NINE

DEALING WITH THE WORKS OF THE FLESH – GALATIANS 5:19–21

It's interesting to note how Christians accuse, and blame the devil for things he is not responsible for. We need to really discipline ourselves by walking in the spirit, rather than the flesh. The scriptures says in,

Galatians 5:19-21

> 19*Now the works of the flesh are manifest, which are these; Adultery, fornication, uncleanness, lasciviousness,*
>
> 20*Idolatry, witchcraft, hatred, variance, emulations, wrath, strife, seditions, heresies,*
>
> 21*Envyings, murders, drunkenness, revellings, and such like: of the which I tell you before, as I have also told you in time past, that they which do such things shall not inherit the kingdom of God.*

Verse 19 above says "*Now the works of the flesh are...*" It didn't say, "*Now the works of the devil are...*" Look at the long list, and see that what a lot of Christians call the work of the devil is not. Perhaps people don't read their Bible well to find out the truth, or they simply want to ignore the truth and blame the devil for every mishap. But this should not be so. We need to accept responsibility for our own mistakes. This is the only way we can grow, and become mature Christians.

After looking at the long list above, it's important to do a honest self-examination, and identify those works of the flesh that needs to be dealt with in your life now, then go ahead to start doing the right things to fix them. No procrastination. Remember, the last part of verse 21 above says that, "*...they which do such things shall not inherit the kingdom of God.*" That's talking about heaven.

HOW TO DEAL WITH THE WORKS OF THE FLESH

One main thing to do in order to deal with the works of the flesh is to walk in the spirit. ***Galatians 5:16*** says, "*This I say then, Walk in the Spirit, and ye shall not fulfil the lust of the flesh.*" Some of the things we have to do in order to walk in the spirit include to do Bible study, meditate, and practice what the Bible says because it's the sword of the spirit according to Ephesians 6:17. We also have to pray, praise, and fellowship with other believers. It's also important to keep on abstaining from sin.

It's also vital to keep on disciplining yourself. ***1 Corinthians 9:27*** says, "*But I keep under my body, and bring it into subjection: lest that by any means, when I have preached to others, I myself should be a castaway.*" Apostle Paul says in this scripture that he disciplines his body. We also have to do same as Christians by saying no to the works of the flesh no matter how tempting they may appear to be. Be in full control as a Christian. It can be done because we are more than conquerors, and overcomers in Jesus' name. Amen!

CHAPTER TEN

GOD HEALS EMOTIONAL PAINS – PSALM 147:3

There is no kind of emotional pain God does not heal. God heals relationship breakdown, depression, stress, business failure, barrenness, sicknesses, addictions and much more.

Psalms 147:3

> *"He healeth the broken in heart, and bindeth up their wounds."*

In order to receive healing from God, it's important that we also position ourselves well to receive it by doing the following:

1. You have to believe and trust God to heal you.
2. Pray and read healing scriptures regularly.
3. Stop complaining about the emotional pain or sickness.
4. Keep on thanking and praising God.
5. Allow time for healing to take place and manifest.
6. Repent of your sins.
7. Keep thinking, speaking, and acting positively.

Before the woman with the issue of blood for twelve years received her healing, she believed within herself that when she touches the garment of Jesus, she will be made whole, and it was so. ***Matthew 9:20–22*** says,

> [20]*And, behold, a woman, which was diseased with an issue of blood twelve years, came behind him, and touched the hem of his garment:*

> [21]*For she said within herself, If I may but touch his garment, I shall be whole.*
>
> [22]*But Jesus turned him about, and when he saw her, he said, Daughter, be of good comfort; thy faith hath made thee whole. And the woman was made whole from that hour.*

It is absolutely vital that you believe, and totally trust in God to heal you in order to receive your healing. No doubting! The reason why some people probably don't cast their burdens on Jesus is because they are not aware of the awesome power of God to deliver and heal those who are in bondage.

Psalms 147:3

> *"He healeth the broken in heart, and bindeth up their wounds."*

To be shattered and broken emotionally should never be the end of life. We are to primarily learn from the experience of whatever made us shattered and use it positively to forge ahead in life. Don't be ashamed to share your pains with others because the pain adds its own beauty to your life. The trials have a role to play in our life and the life of others that's why God allowed it in the first place. I have seen new ministries being born out of the pain people have been through and they now use their experiences to inspire and help others. For example, a person who has been through turbulent trials in marriage could end up having marriage ministry counseling and inspiring other people in marriage. Use the trials you have been through to help others. Be encouraged today and know that God is a specialist in fixing broken hearts. He is the potter and we are the clay. Cast your burdens unto Jesus for He cares for you. Your miracle is now. Believe it and see it manifest in Jesus' name.

CHAPTER ELEVEN

WEEP NO MORE – LUKE 7:13

The Most High God has sent me to you to say WEEP NO MORE.

For I have seen your cries.
For I have seen your tears.
For I have seen your sorrows.
For I have seen your challenges.
For I have seen your pains.
And your time has come to be made whole in Jesus' name.

The Bible says in ***Psalms 42:3***, *"My tears have been my meat day and night, while they continually say unto me, Where is thy God?"* The Psalmist says in this scripture that he wept so much to the extent that his tears became food for him all day. And people now ask, *"Where is thy God?"*

Perhaps you are currently going through storms, afflictions, weeping, and tears. Once again, the Most High God has sent me to you saying weep no more. God has seen your tears. And He is working behind the scenes to perfect all that concerns you in Jesus' name. Shout Amen!

Luke 7:11-16

> 11 *And it came to pass the day after, that he went into a city called Nain; and many of his disciples went with him, and much people.*
>
> 12 *Now when he came nigh to the gate of the city, behold, there was a dead man carried out, the only son of his mother, and she was a widow: and much people of the city was with her.*

13And when the Lord saw her, he had compassion on her, and said unto her, Weep not.

14And he came and touched the bier: and they that bare him stood still. And he said, Young man, I say unto thee, Arise.

15And he that was dead sat up, and began to speak. And he delivered him to his mother.

16And there came a fear on all: and they glorified God, saying, That a great prophet is risen up among us; and, That God hath visited his people.

What can be more devastating than for a widow (somebody who has already lost her husband) to also lose her only son? Ah! Satan is cruel. But I thank God for my Lord Jesus. He appeared on the scene and the dead man came back to life. As God's Anointed, and in the powerful name of Jesus, I declare as follows:

No more weeping.
No more crying.
No more sorrowing.
No more storms.
No more afflictions.
No more shame.
No more disappointments.
Shout Amen!

Psalms 30:5

"For his anger endureth but a moment; in his favour is life: weeping may endure for a night, but joy cometh in the morning."

I have come to announce to you that your weeping is over in Jesus' name. Receive your permanent joy in Jesus' name. Amen!

Finally, read what the scripture says below.

Psalms 71:21

> *"Thou shalt increase my greatness, and comfort me on every side."*

I prophesy to you today that in the name of Jesus Christ of Nazareth, all your weeping shall effectively be turned into greatness, and the God of all comfort shall comfort you indeed in Jesus' name. Shout Amen!

CHAPTER TWELVE

JUST DO IT!

Some Christians argue, challenge, and twist the obvious truth in the Bible to suit their rascally lifestyle. They rebel and blatantly disobey the Word of God. They also argue with their Pastor's teaching. They attack the truth, and hold on to lies. Yet they wonder why they are not prospering. The obvious truth is that God likes obedience to His Word, and reward is normally based on obedience. Let's look at what their response will be to the following Bible references or preaching.

GIVE YOUR TITHE – Their response will be, "Oh tithing has been abolished. That's Old Testament." My friend, what about Matthew 23:23, and Hebrews 7:1–10 in the New Testament that talked about tithe?

MARRY ONLY ONE WIFE – Their response will be, "But King Solomon had 700 wives and 300 concubines. Abraham and David also had more than one wife." They don't want to know the Bible says in the New Testament that a Christian should have only one wife. And that polygamy is not allowed. Bigamy is also an offence.

DON'T FORNICATE – Their response will be, "How will I just marry without making love? How will I know whether the person is good in bed or not? Ah! I need to test it first." Hey! My friend, ***1 Corinthians 6:18*** says, *"Flee fornication."* You've got to marry the bone of your bone and the flesh of your flesh by faith, and by God's leading and guidance.

DON'T DRINK ALCOHOL – Their response will be, "But Jesus turned water to wine. And Paul told Timothy to take wine." They will not make reference to Proverbs 20:1 that says wine is a mocker, and strong drink is raging.

COME TO CHURCH – Their response will be, "Oh church is in the heart. And we are the church and not the physical building." My friend, Jesus went to church regularly. See Luke 4:16. Jesus loved the church. See Ephesians 5:25. See also Hebrews 10:25.

SPEAK IN TONGUES – They will tell you, "That's rubbish. How can I be talking or praying like a mad person?" My friend, it is there in 1 Corinthians 14 that Christians should speak in tongues.

SUBMIT TO YOUR HUSBAND – Their response will be, "Ephesians 5:21 says we should submit to one another in the fear of the Lord. So he has to submit to me too. We are equal." My friend, 1 Corinthians 11:3 says the husband is the head of the wife. And Ephesians 5:22 specifically says wives should submit to their own husbands. And Genesis 3:16 says the husband has to rule the wife.

GIVE QUALITY OFFERINGS TO GOD – Their response will be, "Nobody can deceive me anymore. Show me the God you said I should give my money to. The money is simply for the Pastor to enrich himself. Therefore, I will give a few coins." My friend, God is a spirit so you can't see Him with your physical eyes, yet He exists. He is omnipresent, and this means He is present everywhere. Malachi 1:6 says you should not give peanuts to God. And King Solomon gave quality sacrifice to God in 1 Kings 3:3–5.

It's important for us to understand that God established His commandments for our own good, and also to ensure order. The commandments are things He knows we can keep, and they are not grievous. Read how Apostle John put it in ***1 John 5:3***, *"For this is the love of God, that we keep his commandments: and his commandments are not grievous."*

This message is aimed at achieving one main thing – to avoid arguing with the truth in the Word of God. If the Bible says it, go on and act on it by faith because it is authentic. When I first wrote this message some years ago and posted it on Facebook, it attracted a lot of likes and positive comments indicating that it touched the hearts of people. Hopefully, it will also minister to you.

John 2:5

> *"His mother saith unto the servants, Whatsoever he saith unto you, do it."*

Just do it!

CHAPTER THIRTEEN

THE NAME OF JESUS – ACTS 4:12

The name of Jesus is the name above all names, and it is a powerful tool in the hand of every Christian to pray with, fight battles, and conquer. In order for the name of Jesus to work for you ***effectively***, you must:

1. Be a born again Christian.
2. Have a personal revelation of the power and authority in the name of Jesus.
3. Have a personal relationship with Jesus.
4. Use the name by faith.
5. Use the name with authority. You don't ***beg*** but you ***command*** as you use the name.
6. When you beg you may not get result, but when you command situations and circumstances using the name of Jesus, you get results most times and instantly in some cases.

Acts 4:12

> *"Neither is there salvation in any other: for there is none other name under heaven given among men, whereby we must be saved."*

The name of Jesus Christ is special. He is the only begotten son of the Most High God, the anointed One, Messiah, and Alpha and Omega. He is part of the Godhead or Trinity. Your salvation is guaranteed in His name. Amen!

The name of Jesus is so powerful to the extent that He stated in the scripture below that we should ask whatsoever we desire in His name, and He will do it. But it is important that we are not to ask for evil things. For example, you cannot ask Jesus to help you succeed as you go to rob a bank. That's evil, and Jesus will never grant that. We are meant to ask for any promise of God written in the Bible, and also ask by faith, and He will do it.

John 14:13

> *"And whatsoever ye shall ask in my name, that will I do, that the Father may be glorified in the Son."*

According to the scripture below, Christians are to pray in the name of Jesus to God the Father. You are not to pray in the name of God or the Holy Ghost. And when you pray using the name of Jesus, your request is guaranteed by His grace. Situations and circumstances are bound to bow. I have used the name of Jesus many times to pray and people got delivered and healed. There is tremendous power in the name of Jesus. Use it confidently. No shaking!

Philippians 2:9–11

> 9 *Wherefore God also hath highly exalted him, and given him a name which is above every name:*
>
> 10 *That at the name of Jesus every knee should bow, of things in heaven, and things in earth, and things under the earth;*
>
> 11 *And that every tongue should confess that Jesus Christ is Lord, to the glory of God the Father.*

Acts 19:13–17

> 13 *Then certain of the vagabond Jews, exorcists, took upon them to call over them which had evil spirits the name of the Lord Jesus, saying, We adjure you by Jesus whom Paul preacheth.*
>
> 14 *And there were seven sons of one Sceva, a Jew, and chief of the priests, which did so.*
>
> 15 *And the evil spirit answered and said, Jesus I know, and Paul I know; but who are ye?*

> [16]*And the man in whom the evil spirit was leaped on them, and overcame them, and prevailed against them, so that they fled out of that house naked and wounded.*
>
> [17]*And this was known to all the Jews and Greeks also dwelling at Ephesus; and fear fell on them all, and the name of the Lord Jesus was magnified.*

When a person does not satisfy some, or all of the above six points, (How to effectively use the name of Jesus Christ), they turn out to be like the seven sons of Sceva. The name of Jesus did not work for them.

My prayer is that anytime we genuinely use the name of Jesus Christ by faith,
Sicknesses and diseases shall bow and be destroyed.
Chains and afflictions shall be destroyed and terminated.
There shall be open doors of favour.
There shall be miracles.
And great testimonies shall abound in the name of Jesus Christ of Nazareth.

CHAPTER FOURTEEN

THERE IS SO MUCH GREATNESS IN YOU

You are excellent.
You are amazing.
You are a superstar.
You are extraordinary.
You are fearfully and wonderfully made.
He that is in you is greater than he that's in the world.
You are born again to always win.
You are an overcomer.
You are more than a conqueror.
You are the head and not the tail.
You are above only.
The kingdom of God is within you.
You are created in Christ Jesus unto good works.
You have the authority to tread upon serpents and scorpions, and it shall not hurt you.
No weapon formed against you shall ever prosper.
Your path is like the shining light that shines brighter and brighter unto the perfect day.
You are created for signs and wonders.
You are created to do exploits.
You are blessed with all spiritual blessings.
God has made you to be superb and absolutely great.
Jesus has come to give you life, and give it to you more abundantly.
Don't believe anything less.
Don't let anyone talk you out of who God says you are in the Bible.
There is so much greatness in you! Begin to manifest it in Jesus' name. Amen!

CHAPTER FIFTEEN

DARE INTO THE UNKNOWN – HEBREWS 11:8

Hebrews 11:8

> *"By faith Abraham, when he was called to go out into a place which he should after receive for an inheritance, obeyed; and he went out, not knowing whither he went."*

Abraham dared into the unknown by faith. When God called him, he obeyed, and went out not even knowing where he went. To dare into the unknown involves:

1. Following God's leading and trying something new by faith.
2. Faith simply means acting on the Word of God fearlessly, believing it will yield the promised results.
3. Take some meaningful decisions based on the promises of God.
4. Leaving your comfort zone.
5. Fighting your fears by confronting and boldly doing those things you fear.
6. Most times the things we fear never happen.
7. Take bold steps and change things that has stagnated your progress.
8. Psychologists recommend that we should try out those things that are scary because they help us grow.
9. Perhaps you should even travel out and go on an adventure and experience new things. Go for a prayer retreat in a secluded place. Climb a mountain. Go for a camping. Take a long walk.
10. Stop or start something that you believe can move you into your next level in glory.

Hebrews 11:8

> *"By faith Abraham, when he was called to go out into a place which he should after receive for an inheritance, obeyed; and he went out, not knowing whither he went."*

Dare into the unknown. Try something new and make new discoveries. Your inheritance may be there. It's exciting to try new things!

CHAPTER SIXTEEN

PROPHETIC ACTION FOR YOU – OPERATION SHAKE IT OFF – ACTS 28:3–5

Acts 28:3–5

> [3]*And when Paul had gathered a bundle of sticks, and laid them on the fire, there came a viper out of the heat, and fastened on his hand.*
>
> [4]*And when the barbarians saw the venomous beast hang on his hand, they said among themselves,* No *doubt this man is a murderer, whom, though he hath escaped the sea, yet vengeance suffereth not to live.*
>
> [5]*And he shook off the beast into the fire, and felt no harm.*

The Bible tells us in verse 5 above that the Apostle Paul shook off the snake that entangled his hand into fire and he was not harmed.

Hey! Enough is enough! It's prophetic action time. Begin to shake your hand and entire body as you declare as follows:

> Every serpentine spirit, I shake you off into fire.
> Sicknesses, I shake you off into fire.
> Diseases, I shake you off into fire.
> Debts, I shake you off into fire.
> Poverty, I shake you off into fire.
> Shame, I shake you off into fire.
> Disappointment, I shake you off into fire.
> Unemployment, I shake you off into fire.
> Immigration challenges, I shake you off into fire.

> Loneliness, I shake you off into fire.
> Sorrow, weeping, and crying I shake you off into fire.
> Barrenness, I shake you off into fire.
> Every evil of the enemy, I shake you off into the fire of the Holy Ghost to die and burn to ashes in the name of Jesus Christ of Nazareth.

Your time has come to be free, and free indeed. Apostle Paul was not harmed. Therefore, you shall not be harmed. Get ready to share your testimony. The angels of the Lord are at work right now to effect all round victory in Jesus' name. Amen!

CHAPTER SEVENTEEN

SIN MAY NOT BE THE REASON FOR BONDAGE – JOHN 9:3

Most times when somebody is facing difficult trials, and experiencing heavy bondage, we are quick to think, or conclude that it is a result of the person's ***sin***. But the truth remains that sin may not necessarily be the reason for bondage. Please stop tormenting yourself by feeling guilty, and free your mind. Let's read below the conversation between Jesus and His disciples.

QUESTION

John 9:1-2

> [1]*And as Jesus passed by, he saw a man which was blind from his birth.*
>
> [2]*And his disciples asked him, saying, Master, who did sin, this man, or his parents, that he was born blind?*

ANSWER

John 9:3

> *"Jesus answered, neither hath this man sinned, nor his parents: but that the works of God should be made manifest in him."*

Jesus made it clear in the answer He gave the disciples that neither the man nor his parents sinned to make the man blind, but that the works of God should be made manifest. There are trials we are going through today which God has allowed because He wants to do something unique in our life and for His name to be praised and glorified. You are certainly not going through the trials because of any sin you committed.

I am not writing this message to promote sin. God forbid! But I am writing in line with the Word of God, to say you should stop feeling guilty that your sin is responsible for all the afflictions you go through in life. Your sin may not be responsible after all. When I first wrote this message and posted it on my Facebook some years ago, a young man rang me to thank me, saying that as he read this article a big burden was lifted off his shoulders, and he felt a huge relief and so much peace. According to him, he has been passing through terrible trials, and he has been walking about in pain feeling guilty about the sin he committed, and he believed he was going through trials because of the sin. But he was immediately delivered by this powerful article when he read it and believed the message. Stop judging yourself negatively. Now, this again is not a licence to sin. But thank God the Holy Spirit is in us to prompt and help us always.

John 9:3

> *"Jesus answered, neither hath this man sinned, nor his parents: but that the works of God should be made manifest in him."*

Please move on and enjoy your life to the fullest knowing, and expecting the works of God to be made manifest in your life, rather than focusing all day on what may turn out not to be your sin, and hindering yourself unnecessarily. God bless you abundantly in Jesus' name. Amen!

CHAPTER EIGHTEEN

IT WILL NOT RUN OUT IN JESUS' NAME. AMEN!

No matter how tough things may appear to be right now, simply have a positive mentality and believe that you will never run out of supply. God is the great provider. And He will give you this day, and forever your daily bread. Shout Amen!

I am writing this message to encourage you to have faith and trust God. Give up all fears the devil may be throwing at you now. Firmly connect and trust God. Remember, the just shall live by his faith –Habakkuk 2:4.

Your contract will not run out in Jesus' name. Amen!
Your money will not run out in Jesus' name. Amen!
Your food will not run out in Jesus' name. Amen!

The widow of Zarephath thought she was going to run out of food. But the God of miracles showed up for her with abundance. Read what she said in ***1 Kings 17:12***, "*And she said, As the LORD thy God liveth, I have not a cake, but an handful of meal in a barrel, and a little oil in a cruse: and, behold, I am gathering two sticks, that I may go in and dress it for me and my son, that we may eat it, and die.*" What she thought was going to be her last meal did not run out after the Man of God, Elijah was ministered to.

In 2 Kings 4:1–7, another widow thought it was all over for her and her two sons. Again, the Most High God manifested, and her little oil was miraculously multiplied. As a servant of the Most High God, I declare that the Lord will also appear for you with a pleasant surprise. That little food, money, joy, and peace you have now shall be multiplied miraculously. It will not run out in Jesus' name. Amen! The Bible declares in ***Philippians 4:19***, *"But my God shall supply all your need according to his riches in glory by Christ Jesus."*

I have been through trials and wilderness experiences, and one thing I discovered about God is that He will always sustain you with manna. Your daily bread is guaranteed no matter how tough things may seem to be. Even when you think you now have the last meal, He will provide more miraculously. Just keep trusting Him.

Jesus said in ***John 10:10***, *"The thief cometh not, but for to steal, and to kill, and to destroy: I am come that they might have life, and that they might have it more abundantly."* Receive abundance of food, money, joy, and peace by faith in Jesus' name. As a born again Christian, have faith in God that He has come to supply all your need, as well as give you the goodies of life more abundantly. You should be excited to know this. Just keep declaring that you have abundance of every good thing. Never talk negatively. Be positive!

CHAPTER NINETEEN

IMAGINATIONS – 2 CORINTHIANS 10:5

Your imagination is the only limit to what you can hope to have in the future. Nothing else can be a barrier. The limitation you put on your mind is the only thing that can stop you in life. All limitations are self-imposed through negative imaginations and thinking. The only limit to your realisation of tomorrow will be your pains of yesterday, and your doubts of today, but you must not remain static. You must boldly go beyond your limitations.

You are confined only to the walls you build yourself because there are no limits to the glorious future which lies before you. No limits! No excuses! I challenge you now to dismantle the negative boundaries of your imagination and stop putting limits on your life. We have two types of imaginations.

1. Positive imaginations
2. Negative imaginations

Both kinds of imaginations are formed in our minds. And it is entirely our choice to paint the right or wrong imaginations. The kind of imagination we form in our mind is a reflection of our life externally. What you feed the mind as input is what it will process and you will get a corresponding output.

CASTING DOWN NEGATIVE IMAGINATIONS

2 Corinthians 10:5

> *"Casting down imaginations, and every high thing that exalteth itself against the knowledge of God, and bringing into captivity every thought to the obedience of Christ;"*

To cast down simply means to get rid of. Negative imaginations are unhealthy, and therefore, must be thrashed. Simply don't waste your precious time dwelling on negative things or worrying unnecessarily.

Proverbs 23:7

> *"For as he thinketh in his heart, so is he: Eat and drink, saith he to thee; but his heart is not with thee."*

As a person thinks in his heart, so is the person now. Not will be. Today, delete all negative thinking, and replace them with healthy positive thinking.

Cast down imaginations of sickness
Cast down imaginations of generational curses
Cast down imaginations of witches and snakes pursuing you everywhere
Cast down imaginations of death
Cast down imaginations of poverty
Cast down imaginations of examination, career, or business failure
Cast down imaginations of loneliness and marriage failure
Cast down imaginations of stagnation

SOLUTION FOR NEGATIVE IMAGINATIONS

1. Start renewing your mind with the Word of God. See Romans 12:2.
2. Deliberately start thinking, speaking, and acting positively. Yes! You can do it.
   Picture it in your mind that you are healthy
   Picture it in your mind that you are blessed and highly favoured
   Picture it in your mind that you will live long
   Picture it in your mind that you are successful and prosperous
   Picture it in your mind that you are intelligent and will pass your examination
   Picture it in your mind that you will marry that handsome man or beautiful woman you like

Picture it in your mind that you will own that nice car, and house you like.

3. Print out pictures of what you want. For example, car and house and place them in your bedroom where you can see them regularly. It will help establish positive thinking.
4. Associate yourself with people who are positive in their thinking, beliefs, speaking, and actions. As you do all these, your positive imaginations will be fully established and start manifesting and cause you to soar like an eagle. God bless you.

CHAPTER TWENTY

ENCOURAGE YOURSELF – 1 SAMUEL 30:6

1 Samuel 30:6

> *"And David was greatly distressed; for the people spake of stoning him, because the soul of all the people was grieved, every man for his sons and for his daughters: but David encouraged himself in the Lord his God."*

The above scripture says, "*And David was greatly distressed...*" But the good news is that in spite of the great distress, David did not do anything silly or stupid. He did not turn to alcohol, hard drugs, or womanising. He did not commit suicide or murder. Instead, the Bible says, "*... but David encouraged himself in the Lord his God.*"

What do you do when you are greatly distressed? What do you do when things go terribly wrong and all hope seems to be lost? What do you do when everyone including friends, family, colleagues, church members, club members, and neighbours are not giving you any attention and support in time of distress? Sit down and cry, and engage yourself in a pity party? Say, "God forbid, and I forbid!" It's time to encourage yourself in the Lord.

The first and major help you will get in time of distress is certainly going to come from you believing and trusting God to help you out. Your personal conviction that you will get out of the pit with miry clay is important coupled with your attempts and efforts to get out. This will now get all things to work together in your good for divine connections to orchestrate help for you to possibly get help through men, but you must initiate positive action plans.

HOW TO ENCOURAGE YOURSELF IN THE LORD

In time of great distress, the first thing to do is to reach out for your life manual, the Holy Bible and start studying and meditating on scriptures. Use your concordance to highlight appropriate scriptures you can use to deal with the issues you are facing. Combine this with prayers, praise and worship unto God while ensuring you keep abstaining from sin. Keep listening to powerful messages preached by notable Pastors, and fellowship with other believers regularly. Speak and prophesy good positive things into your life by making positive confessions. Also read relevant Christian books. Always think positively, believing and trusting God, while you picture God helping you out of the great distress.

Finally, always remember *"...but David encouraged himself in the lord his God."* It's your turn to encourage yourself in the Lord. Nobody will do it for you. It is, "Do it yourself" (DIY).

CHAPTER TWENTY-ONE

HAVING THE RIGHT ATTITUDE

Two men employed by the same company and doing exactly the same type of job were made redundant the same day by the company. The company explained that they were no longer needed because of lack of production raw materials.

Mr A burst out into a rage and tongue lashed his boss and the entire management of the company. He felt the redundancy meant the end of having a good life - No more money for him and his family. He was so furious and bitter that he couldn't see God making a way for him to get another job. Wrong attitude!

On the other hand, Mr B calmly encouraged himself and would not speak against anyone in the company. He believed God for a much better job and opportunities because when one door closes, many better doors opens. He told himself he will even take up a voluntary job anywhere for a start. Right attitude!

Mr A ended up not having another job for years and he blamed everybody, his company, witches and wizards for his bad luck. He did not blame himself. He is faultless, Mr Perfect.

Mr B got another job after just two weeks. His friend who worked for another company just called him and told him about existing vacancy in their company, and he applied and was asked to start immediately. This goes to show that having the right attitude can contribute to our huge progress and success in life.

HOW TO HAVE THE RIGHT ATTITUDE

Firstly, to have the right attitude means to give God thanks in every situation. The Bible says in **1 *Thessalonians 5:18***, *"In everything give thanks: for this is the will of God in Christ Jesus concerning you."* To thank God in everything means to ignore and forget the bad thing that happened, and then focus on the good things happening to you. Forget the former things and God will do a new thing. Thank God you are alive and well.

Secondly, to have the right attitude also means to rejoice always. ***Philippians 4:4*** says, *"Rejoice in the Lord alway: and again I say, Rejoice."* We are to rejoice at all times thus says the Word of God. Our rejoicing should not be limited to only when we get a new job, have a promotion at work, make more money in our business, pass our examinations, buy a new car or house, marry, or have a new born baby. No! Rejoice always. Prophet Habakkuk stated below that he will always rejoice whether things are good or bad. Right attitude!

Habakkuk 3:17–19

> *17. Although the fig tree shall not blossom, neither shall fruit be in the vines; the labour of the olive shall fail, and the fields shall yield no meat; the flock shall be cut off from the fold, and there shall be no herd in the stalls: 18. Yet I will rejoice in the Lord, I will joy in the God of my salvation. 19. The Lord God is my strength, and he will make my feet like hindsfeet, and he will make me to walk upon mine high places. To the chief singer on my stringed instruments.*

In the beginning of his book, Prophet Habakkuk complained so much. But nothing good happened because to complain is to have the wrong attitude. He later started rejoicing - Hab. 3:18. Right attitude!

Thirdly, to have the right attitude is to choose not to let any challenge get through to you. Insulate yourself.

2 Corinthians 4:8–9

> *8 We are troubled on every side, yet not distressed; we are perplexed, but not in despair;*
>
> *9 Persecuted, but not forsaken; cast down, but not destroyed;*

My prayer today and forever is that no matter the challenges we may face in life the Lord will grant us the grace and wisdom to have the right attitude and also come off victorious in Jesus' name. Amen!

CHAPTER TWENTY-TWO

ENDURE AFFLICTIONS – 2 TIMOTHY 2:3

As born again Christians, we are made with supernatural material. We are fearfully and wonderfully made. We are more than conquerors, and overcomers. Hence, we are to withstand the fiery darts of the enemy with our shield of faith, and endure afflictions as good soldiers of Christ. Perhaps you are facing a lot of challenges today, to the extent that you may be asking, "How, and when will all these afflictions be over?" The message for you is endure afflictions. God is working behind the scenes to grant you all round victory in Jesus' name. Amen! How do I know you will come out of all your challenges victoriously? Because ***Psalms 34:19–20*** says:

> [19]*Many are the afflictions of the righteous: but the Lord delivereth him out of them all.*
>
> [20]*He keepeth all his bones: not one of them is broken.*

My friend, give God the glory first for His Word knowing that your victory is guaranteed regarding whatever challenge you may be facing today. Sing praises to Him, laugh and dance.

THINGS TO NOTE ABOUT AFFLICTION

1. **Afflictions will come, but you will overcome them.**

John 16:33

> *"These things I have spoken unto you, that in me ye might have peace. In the world ye shall have tribulation: but be of good cheer; I have overcome the world."*

Jesus spoke these words. He said we shall face tribulations (afflictions) in this world, but we should cheer up because He has overcome them for us. Amen! So, cheer up now my friend.

2. **Afflictions don't last forever. You pass through them.**

Isaiah 43:2 says,

> *"When thou passest through the water, I will be with thee; and through the rivers, they shall not overflow thee: when thou walkest through the fire, thou shalt not be burned; neither shall the flame kindle upon thee."*

Anything that has a beginning must have an end including afflictions. No condition is permanent. So, my friend, pass through those afflictions knowing fully well that God is with you, and the afflictions will definitely be over one day. Amen!

3. **God will not permit any affliction that will overwhelm you.**

1 Corinthians 10:13

> *"There hath no temptation taken you but such as is common to man: but God is faithful, who will not suffer you to be tempted above that ye are able; but will with the temptation also make a way to escape, that ye may be able to bear it."*

Afflictions are customised. The ones you go through are specifically designed for only you. The same goes for me. The good news is that the afflictions you go through are such that they are common to men. Not totally strange. And God allows it because He knows you can bear it successfully. Also, there is always a way of escape for temptations we go through.

4. **Affliction time is training time.**

Psalms 119:71-72

> 71 *It is good for me that I have been afflicted; that I might learn thy statutes.*

> [72]*The law of thy mouth is better unto me than thousands of gold and silver.*

The Psalmist is saying in the above verses that it was good that he was afflicted because it gave him the opportunity to read his Bible. Therefore, affliction period is a time to study the Word of God and grow in wisdom – Training!

5. **Afflictions bring forth promotion and glory of God.**

After Shadrach, Meshach, and Abednego (SMA) successfully went through the fire (affliction), the Bible recorded in ***Daniel 3:30*** *"Then the king promoted Shadrach, Meshach, and Abednego, in the province of Babylon."* Your promotion is guaranteed after affliction in Jesus' name. Amen!

2 Corinthians 4:17

> *"For our light affliction, which is but for a moment, worketh for us a far more exceeding and eternal weight of glory;"*

Glory be to God. The afflictions we go through today will only bring glory to us and God in Jesus' name. Amen!

6. **You must be ready to endure afflictions.**

2 Timothy 2:3

> *"Thou therefore endure hardness, as a good soldier of Jesus Christ."*

Only the good soldiers of Christ triumph over afflictions. Only bold people who are full of faith and belief in Christ Jesus triumph over afflictions. The feeble minded, fearful, and cowards crumble in afflictions. My friend, roll up your sleeves and be ready to fight your way through those challenges as a good soldier of Christ.

7. **Note that you must not complain during afflictions.**

Job went through series of afflictions. He lost everything he had. Yes, everything! But he did not complain or blame God by asking "why me?"

Job 1:22 says,

"In all this Job sinned not, nor charged God foolishly."

Jesus Christ of Nazareth was afflicted seriously for our sake. And the Bible declared in ***Isaiah 53:7*** *"He was oppressed, and he was afflicted, yet he opened not his mouth: he is brought as a lamb to the slaughter, and as a sheep before her shearers is dumb, so he openeth not his mouth."*–To complain. This is what to "endure affliction" means, and that's what gives victory. Instead of complaining, open your mouth and give God all the praise and glory.

PRAYER – My prayer for you today is that the Lord will see you through any challenge you may be facing in Jesus' name. God will endow you with the wisdom to overcome every challenge. With your eyes you will see every enemy, and challenge crumble and be destroyed in the mighty name of Jesus. I declare permanent victory for you in Jesus' name. Amen!

CHAPTER TWENTY-THREE

THE MAJORITY IS NOT ALWAYS RIGHT.

Always stand for what is right, honest, and true in line with the scriptures even if you have to stand alone. People may call you names, and maybe see you as old fashioned, but the truth is that the Most High God will always vindicate you because of His Word. People including even Christians indulge in things that are not right, acceptable, or below the standard of the Bible. They do wrong things, and their defence is that others are doing it. And that is totally unacceptable. As Christians, Jesus is our role model and He is the One we should be looking up to, and not any man. Let the Bible also be your accepted standard to live your life.

Should a Christian lie, steal, fornicate, and prostitute just because others are doing it? Or should a Christian commit murder, become a gangster, become a fraudster or exhibit all manner of evil character just because others are doing it? Are you others? Remember, God is a God to every individual believer. He relates with every believer on their own level. Therefore, it will not be right to join others to do evil. Read below what the Bible says in

Exodus 23:2

> *"Thou shalt not follow a multitude to do evil; neither shalt thou speak in a cause to decline after many to wrest judgment:"*

It is wrong and evil in the sight of the Lord to join the multitude to do evil. Always stand for integrity. And this means you don't have to endorse evil in any way. Read again what the Bible says in

2 Corinthians 6:14–17

> [14]*Be ye not unequally yoked together with unbelievers: for what fellowship hath righteousness with unrighteousness? and what communion hath light with darkness?*
>
> [15]*And what concord hath Christ with Belial? or what part hath he that believeth with an infidel?*
>
> [16]*And what agreement hath the temple of God with idols? for ye are the temple of the living God; as God hath said, I will dwell in them, and walk in them; and I will be their God, and they shall be my people.*
>
> [17]*Wherefore come out from among them, and be ye separate, saith the Lord, and touch not the unclean thing; and I will receive you.*

PROPHET MICAIAH. (2 Chronicles 18:1-34 & 1Kings 22:1–35)

Prophet Micaiah is a perfect example of someone in the Bible who did not follow a multitude to do evil. He stood alone against four hundred prophets (1 VS 400). The four hundred prophets gave a positive prophesy that God will deliver Ramothgilead into King Ahab's hand. But Prophet Micaiah damned the consequences of being punished and went ahead and gave a negative prophesy that King Ahab will not come back from the Ramothgilead war alive. He was immediately imprisoned. But eventually, the Lord vindicated him as King Ahab died in the war as he prophesied. That's integrity. Do you accept bribe to pervert justice? That's evil! Do you refuse to stand for the truth because of fear of what men will do to you? Remember, if God be for you, nobody can be against you.

Always remember Prophet Micaiah who stood his ground alone and told the truth in spite of four hundred prophets saying the opposite, any time the devil tries to deceive you to do evil. The majority is not always right. Always choose to do what the Bible says. God bless you.

CHAPTER TWENTY-FOUR

HARD TRUTH – RETALIATION

This is a Holy Spirit inspired message that God has commanded me to deliver. Thus saith the LORD in:

Romans 12:19

> *"Dearly beloved, avenge not yourselves, but rather give place unto wrath: for it is written, Vengeance is mine; I will repay, saith the Lord."*

God is saying, "*Vengeance is mine; I will repay, saith the Lord.*" And this means we should not retaliate. We've got to leave God to deal with those who hurt us. Hallelujah! The pain of serious wounds inflicted on victims can be very serious and unbearable. I have personally been through trials inflicted on me by some wicked folks without revenging. One of the proofs to show we are mature Christians is when we can bear out of love the pain some wicked folks dish out to us. My dear, we are no longer in the era of:

Exodus 21:24–25

> [24]*"Eye for eye, tooth for tooth, hand for hand, foot for foot,"*
>
> [25]*"Burning for burning, wound for wound, stripe for stripe."*

We are now in the era of:

Matthew 5:44

> *"But I say unto you, Love your enemies, bless them that curse you, do good to them that hate you, and pray for them which despitefully use you, and persecute you;"*

Without adequate wisdom and grace of God, Matthew 5:44 will continue to be one of the toughest scriptures in the Bible for babes in Christ, but as you are broken and crushed in your walk with God, you will grow up in love to be a mature Christian who will see Matthew 5:44 as a very easy scripture to practice.

Exodus 14:14 says:

> *"The Lord shall fight for you, and ye shall hold your peace."*

It's so nice to sit back and relax while the Lord fights for us in battle against the adversary. You don't have to raise a finger, yet your victory is guaranteed, because the battle is the Lord's. Your victory is guaranteed over those enemies that trouble you as you effectively allow God to repay them. It's interesting to note that you will always gain far much victory whenever you allow God to fight for you than when you fight the battle on your own. Even when it seems God is not fighting your battles straightaway to repay your enemies, just relax and hold your peace. God is more calculative than you, and He is the only wise God. Relax! The battle is the Lord's.

I see you triumphing over the enemy in Jesus' name. Remember, you are not being a coward, a weakling, or a foolish person by not retaliating. You are only displaying love, maturity, and obedience to His Word, and this is the reason why you will surely overcome those who hurt you. God bless you for hearkening to the voice of the Lord not to retaliate.

CHAPTER TWENTY-FIVE

THE FEAR OF THE LORD

Psalms 111:10

> *"The fear of the Lord is the beginning of wisdom: a good understanding have all they that do his commandments: his praise endureth for ever."*

To fear God does not mean you have to start running away from God because He will bully you and punish you. No! God loves you. He is your Father and friend. We are talking about reverential fear here, and this simply means to know His Word and respect Him by obeying His Word. To fear God also means to detest sin, and also desist from doing anything you believe will make Him angry. For example, you have your earthly biological father, who you live with and you know the things he doesn't like, and you avoid doing them. Similarly, don't do anything the Bible says you shouldn't do because God will not like it.

Psalms 119:11

> *"Thy word have I hid in mine heart, that I might not sin against thee."*

Flood your heart with scriptures so much that whenever there is an issue to deal with, you already have a scripture addressing that issue. Let the Word of God hid in your heart counsel you always. And anytime you know what the Word of God says, and you fail to obey it, you don't fear Him. Again, you don't fear God if you only do the right things because people are watching you. The fear of God means that you do the right things even when no one is watching you in your secret chambers. God is watching you anyway because His presence is everywhere. God knows those who fear Him and He rewards them. You can't fake the fear of God.

BENEFITS OF THE FEAR OF THE LORD

1. THE FEAR OF GOD WILL REVEAL HIS SECRET TO YOU.

Psalms 25:14

> *"The secret of the Lord is with them that fear him; and he will shew them his covenant."*

2. IT WILL PROLONG YOUR DAYS.

Proverbs 10:27

> *"The fear of the Lord prolongeth days: but the years of the wicked shall be shortened."*

3. IT WILL BRING FORTH RICHES

Proverbs 22:4

> *"By humility and the fear of the Lord are riches, and honour, and life."* God will reward you with riches, honour, and life when you fear Him. See also Gen. 22:16-18.

4. CONCLUSION OF THE WHOLE MATTER

Ecclesiastes 12:13

> *"Let us hear the conclusion of the whole matter: fear God, and keep his commandments: for this is the whole duty of man."* God bless you.

CHAPTER TWENTY-SIX

GOD IS BIGGER THAN YOUR CHALLENGE

God is definitely bigger than any challenge we may face in life. That's why the Bible declares that with God all things are possible, including that challenge you may think is massive. No matter how mountainous a challenge may seem to be, when you call upon the Most High God by faith, the challenge will be dealt with swiftly and victoriously.

2 Corinthians 4:17

> *"For our light affliction, which is but for a moment, worketh for us a far more exceeding and eternal weight of glory;"*

The Bible calls our challenges a light affliction which will only last but for a moment. And it will cause the glory of God to show forth in our life. I prophesy right now that you will come out victoriously from whatever challenge you may be going through in Jesus' name. Amen! The songwriter writes, "*I have a very big God o, He's always by side...*"

You can't have a very big God by your side and fail. Amen!

Romans 8:31

> *"What shall we then say to these things? If God be for us, who can be against us?"*

God is on your side. So you can't fail in Jesus' name. Somebody you least expect is praying for you in America that you will be successful. Right now, I'm also encouraging you with this message and the Word of God that you are a winner regarding the challenge you may be facing.

The God that parted the red sea is still alive. The God that provided manna for the Israelites in the wilderness is still alive. The God that created heaven and earth is still alive. God loves you and He will never leave you nor forsake you.

Jeremiah 32:17

> *"Ah Lord God! behold, thou hast made the heaven and the earth by thy great power and stretched out arm, and there is nothing too hard for thee:"*

Nothing is too hard for God including that challenge you may think is big. Cheer up because Jesus has overcome all tribulations on the cross of Calvary.

CHAPTER TWENTY-SEVEN

ETERNAL LIFE

QUESTION

Mark 10:17

> [1]*"And when he was gone forth into the way, there came one running, and kneeled to him, and asked him, Good Master, what shall I do that I may inherit eternal life?"*

ANSWER

Mark 10:18–22

> 18*And Jesus said unto him, Why callest thou me good? there is none good but one, that is, God.*
>
> 19*Thou knowest the commandments, Do not commit adultery, Do not kill, Do not steal, Do not bear false witness, Defraud not, Honour thy father and mother.*
>
> 20*And he answered and said unto him, Master, all these have I observed from my youth.*
>
> 21*Then Jesus beholding him loved him, and said unto him, One thing thou lackest: go thy way, sell whatsoever thou hast, and give to the poor, and thou shalt have treasure in heaven: and come, take up the cross, and follow me.*
>
> 22*And he was sad at that saying, and went away grieved: for he had great possessions.*

I love the above question, and the answer given by Jesus. Don't let anyone deceive you into believing anything different from the answer Jesus gave. Receive salvation by believing and confessing that Jesus is your personal Lord and Saviour, and steadfastly continue to live a holy life, obeying His commandments, and you will eventually find yourself in heaven.

There is absolutely nothing wrong in being wealthy. You can be stupendously wealthy and still make it to heaven having eternal life. Genesis 24:1 tells us that in old age, the Lord had blessed Abraham in all things. That's stupendous wealth. And then in Luke 16:22 we see that Abraham made it to heaven. However, the rich young ruler we discussed above is different. His riches had him. He trusted his money more than in God. That's why he preferred to hold on to his goods, rather than to sell them and give the proceeds to the poor, and receive salvation. He walked away defiantly. How can Jesus ask you to do something and you refuse and walk away? He is probably languishing in hell now.

No matter what anybody does in this world during their lifetime, even if they are the most educated, most wealthy, the wisest or whatever, they have failed woefully if they end up in hell to burn in the lake of fire perpetually. That's why we must focus on heavenly things much more than earthly things. Set your affections on heavenly matters because that's about eternity and there are many mansions there for the children of God.

CHAPTER TWENTY-EIGHT

ARE YOU MORE EARTHLY MINDED OR HEAVENLY MINDED?

To be earthly minded is to concentrate solely on worldly things and these are mainly material things. They include acquiring chains of qualifications, money, cars, houses, lands, and businesses. As good as these things appear to be, they are all perishable, and we cannot take any of these things to the grave when we translate to be with the Lord.

1 Timothy 6:7

> *"For we brought nothing into this world, and it is certain we can carry nothing out."*

On the other hand, to be heavenly minded is to become a born again Christian, walking in the paths of righteousness, holiness, and love. It also means to constantly evangelise, sowing financially to support the work of God, living life to honour God in prayers, praise, worship, and keeping the commandments of God. As you do all these, you become heavenly minded, and this guarantees eternal life. Let's look at a few scriptures below to give us a picture of how being earthly minded compares to being heavenly minded.

Romans 8:6

> *"For to be carnally minded is death; but to be spiritually minded is life and peace."*

Galatians 6:8

> *"For he that soweth to his flesh shall of the flesh reap corruption; but he that soweth to the Spirit shall of the Spirit reap life everlasting."*

Matthew 6:19–20

> [19]*Lay not up for yourselves treasures upon earth, where moth and rust doth corrupt, and where thieves break through and steal:*
>
> [20]*But lay up for yourselves treasures in heaven, where neither moth nor rust doth corrupt, and where thieves do not break through nor steal:*

Mark 8:36

> *"For what shall it profit a man, if he shall gain the whole world, and lose his own soul?"*

From the above scriptures, it is obvious that as good as earthly material things may appear to be, it will suffer corruption or perish. While on the other hand, spiritual things will lead to eternal life. Our stay on earth is temporary. That's why at the end of the day, every Christian will definitely translate to be with the Lord some day, to a permanent place of abode. When you read the book of Revelations chapter 21, you will find a description of heaven as a beautiful place of eternity and every wise believer should channel their whole energy towards making it to heaven.

THINGS TO DO TO MAKE IT TO HEAVEN

To be a born again Christian is not an automatic licence to make it to heaven as some people are erroneously made to believe. Some people after confessing that Jesus is their Lord still go back to their old ways and lifestyle and this ought not to be. This shows that they probably didn't mean their confession that Jesus is their Lord. No conviction! In fact, our making it to heaven is a continuous exercise which includes working out our own salvation with fear and trembling by improving on our habits, character, and being obedient to the commandments of God. The Bible says that people who do the following things cannot inherit the kingdom of God.

Corinthians 6:9–10

> [9]*Know ye not that the unrighteous shall not inherit the kingdom of God? Be not deceived: neither fornicators, nor idolaters, nor adulterers, nor effeminate, nor abusers of themselves with mankind,*
>
> [10]*Nor thieves, nor covetous, nor drunkards, nor revilers, nor extortioners, shall inherit the kingdom of God.*

It's interesting to note that Apostle Paul wrote the above to Christians in the church of Corinth. This goes to prove the fact that salvation is not a one sure deal of confessing that Jesus is Lord and Saviour. It's a continuous exercise of a life of holiness and total obedience unto the Lord. See also Galatians 5:19-21 for a further list of things to stop doing in order to make it to heaven.

WHY WE HAVE TO BE HEAVENLY MINDED.

The best thing that can happen to a believer is for them to end up in heaven. Therefore, set your heart on heavenly things. Heaven is full of the best things you can ever imagine. Jesus says in,

John 14:2

> *"In my Father's house are many mansions: if it were not so, I would have told you. I go to prepare a place for you."*

Whao! There is no kind of mansion we will ever have here on earth that can compare with the heavenly mansions Jesus promised us. Therefore,

Colossians 3:2

> *"Set your affection on things above, not on things on the earth."*

ASSURANCE OF RAPTURE

We have to do a sincere soul searching now, and ask this important question. If there is a rapture now and Jesus appears will I be taken? Be sure you have the assurance of making it to heaven. No one knows when Jesus will come.

Matthew 24:36

> *"But of that day and hour knoweth no man, no, not the angels of heaven, but my Father only."*

In preparation for the coming of our Lord Jesus Christ, it is better to start doing what the scripture below says.

Hebrews 12:14

> *"Follow peace with all men, and holiness, without which no man shall see the Lord:"*

See you in heaven by the special grace of God. God bless you in Jesus' name. Amen!

CHAPTER TWENTY-NINE

WHAT IS FAITH?

Hebrews 11:1

> *"Now faith is the substance of things hoped for, the evidence of things not seen."*

SOME OF THE THINGS TO KNOW ABOUT FAITH

1. Faith is *now*. You don't postpone acting out your faith.
2. Faith is the *substance* or *realisation* of things hoped for.
3. Faith has *evidence* or *conviction* of things not seen.
4. When you say you have faith, you *start acting*. Faith is therefore *active* and not *dormant*.
5. Doubt, unbelief, and fear, does not go with faith that produces. Avoid them.
6. Faith without works is dead. Faith is dead if it does not produce.

James 2:17

> *"Even so faith, if it hath not works, is dead, being alone."*

7. Constantly hearing the Word of God will boost your faith.

Romans 10:17

> *"So then faith cometh by hearing, and hearing by the word of God."*

8. Without faith it is impossible to please God.

Hebrews 11:6

> *"But without faith it is impossible to please him: for he that cometh to God must believe that he is, and that he is a rewarder of them that diligently seek him."*

9. The just shall live by his faith.

Habakkuk 2:4

> *"Behold, his soul which is lifted up is not upright in him: but the just shall live by his faith."*

10. Faith is not necessarily accomplished by physical strength.

Zechariah 4:6

> *"Then he answered and spake unto me, saying, This is the word of the Lord unto Zerubbabel, saying, Not by might, nor by power, but by my spirit, saith the Lord of hosts."*

11. Faith and belief are synonymous. Both are active words.
12. Faith pictures things with the eye of the heart.
13. Every man has a measure of faith.

Romans 12:3

> *"For I say, through the grace given unto me, to every man that is among you, not to think of himself more highly than he ought to think; but to think soberly, according as God hath dealt to every man the measure of faith."*

14. Faith works by love. This means without love faith can't work. They go together.

Galatians 5:6

> *"For in Jesus Christ neither circumcision availeth anything, nor uncircumcision; but faith which worketh by love."*

15. Faith moves mountain.

Matthew 17:20

> *"And Jesus said unto them, Because of your unbelief: for verily I say unto you, If ye have faith as a grain of mustard seed, ye shall say unto this mountain, Remove hence to yonder place; and it shall remove; and nothing shall be impossible unto you."*

16. Any time you believe something and you start acting out your faith with total conviction, what happens is that energy is pulled towards that direction and you start receiving open doors, help from men and God, and other forces of nature to make what you have faith for to happen. The universe begins to cooperate with you to help you. This is simply a mystery hard to explain. You need to start acting out your faith to experience it. I have seen it happen both in my life and in the life of others.

UNDERSTANDING FAITH – PRACTICAL EXAMPLE 1

Years ago, a single woman I know, who believed in God for a husband started acting out her faith. How? First, she settled it in her mentality with full conviction in her spirit that her husband will manifest. And she went ahead and started acting. Secondly, she bought a double bed. She bought a pair of special tea cups, tumblers, cutlery, pyjamas, Bibles, etc. Everything double!

And any time she comes to church, she will leave a Bible on the seat next to her. Initially she had a hard time with ushers who want to put someone on the seat beside her but could not because she will start begging the ushers claiming that the seat is reserved for her husband who will soon manifest. Crazy! People thought she was crazy but the good news is that it was not long Mr Right manifested and she got married. Yeah! That's faith in operation. When you start acting out your faith, people will see you as crazy. But just don't give in when they call you names, or mock you. Don't be distracted. Don't let them puncture your faith. Hold on firmly to your faith until you see the manifestation.

UNDERSTANDING FAITH – PRACTICAL EXAMPLE 2

A woman just got married. No sign of pregnancy. She went shopping for baby boy clothes. She wanted a baby boy. She believed God would give her a baby boy. So she went ahead acting out her faith by buying those baby boy's clothes before pregnancy, and manifestation of the baby boy. Crazy! Yeah! Faith that produces is indeed crazy. The good news is that the Lord honoured this woman's faith and she gave birth to a bouncing baby boy. This is faith in action.

ASSIGNMENT

I'm going to give you a practical assignment regarding this subject of faith. The assignment is that you should start putting your faith into action now regarding whatever you believe God for. Hold on to appropriate scriptures and act as you are led by the Holy Spirit by taking little steps of faith. Act now! God is pleased when you act by faith. You can do it! I am joining my faith with yours. You can do all things through Christ who strengthens you. You are an overcomer. You are more than a conqueror. Act by faith now!

CHAPTER THIRTY

AGGRESSIVE FAITH IN ACTION

Matthew 11:12

> *"And from the days of John the Baptist until now the kingdom of heaven suffereth violence, and the violent take it by force."*

AGGRESSIVE FAITH ALWAYS SAYS NO TO BAD SITUATIONS

Aggressive faith will declare enough is enough! Enter into warfare prayer in tongues. Cry out to God in prayers. Search the scriptures diligently for answers. Go into serious praise and worship sessions. Make a sacrifice of fat offering unto the Lord. Be in church fellowship with other believers. And forcefully snatch that which rightfully belongs to you from the enemy. Your victory and testimony is guaranteed.

Mark 10:46–48

> 46 *And they came to Jericho: and as he went out of Jericho with his disciples and a great number of people, blind Bartimaeus, the son of Timaeus, sat by the highway side begging.*
>
> 47 *And when he heard that it was Jesus of Nazareth, he began to cry out, and say, Jesus, thou Son of David, have mercy on me.*
>
> 48 *And many charged him that he should hold his peace: but he cried the more a great deal, Thou Son of David, have mercy on me.*

Blind Bartimaeus received his sight using aggressive faith. Nobody was able to shut him up. He raised aggressive alarm and caught the attention of Jesus, and received his sight. As you do the same, you will capture Jesus attention, and receive your heart desires.

Genesis 32:24–26

> 24*And Jacob was left alone; and there wrestled a man with him until the breaking of the day.*
>
> 25*And when he saw that he prevailed not against him, he touched the hollow of his thigh; and the hollow of Jacob's thigh was out of joint, as he wrestled with him.*
>
> 26*And he said, Let me go, for the day breaketh. And he said, I will not let thee go, except thou bless me.*

Jacob wrestled with the Angel of God saying, "*...I will not let thee go, except thou bless me.*" He held on to God in an encounter until God blessed him. Aggressive, tenacious faith will tarry in His presence until God releases the blessings.

I heard the story of a man who was unjustly sentenced to seven years imprisonment. He commenced a fast in prison for his immediate release. The prison officials thought he was on hunger strike and became concerned. On his fortieth day of fast, his prayers and praise increased tremendously and a great earthquake of freedom similar to the one in Acts 16:26 that freed Paul and Silas struck and the man was miraculously freed. That's aggressive faith in action.

CHAPTER THIRTY-ONE

COMPARING THE WICKED WITH THE RIGHTEOUS – READ WHAT THE BIBLE SAYS.

1. *Psalms 7:11*

   "God judgeth the righteous, and God is angry with the wicked every day."

2. *Psalms 32:10*

   "Many sorrows shall be to the wicked: but he that trusteth in the Lord, mercy shall compass him about".

3. *Psalms 34:21*

   "Evil shall slay the wicked: and they that hate the righteous shall be desolate."

4. *Psalms 37:17*

   "For the arms of the wicked shall be broken: but the Lord upholdeth the righteous."

5. *Proverbs 10:24*

   "The fear of the wicked, it shall come upon him: but the desire of the righteous shall be granted."

6. *Proverbs 10:25*

   "As the whirlwind passeth, so is the wicked no more: but the righteous is an everlasting foundation."

7. Proverbs 10:27–30

27 *The fear of the Lord prolongeth days: but the years of the wicked shall be shortened.*

28 *The hope of the righteous shall be gladness: but the expectation of the wicked shall perish.*

29 *The way of the Lord is strength to the upright: but destruction shall be to the workers of iniquity.*

30 *The righteous shall never be removed: but the wicked shall not inhabit the earth.*

8. Proverbs 11:5

"The righteousness of the perfect shall direct his way: but the wicked shall fall by his own wickedness."

9. Proverbs 11:8

"The righteous is delivered out of trouble, and the wicked cometh in his stead."

10. Ezekiel 18:20

"The soul that sinneth, it shall die. The son shall not bear the iniquity of the father, neither shall the father bear the iniquity of the son: the righteousness of the righteous shall be upon him, and the wickedness of the wicked shall be upon him."

The above scripture says it all. And you can even do your own personal study and you will find out more scriptures on this subject. Today, choose between being wicked and righteous. The Bible has clearly laid out what will happen to both the wicked and the righteous. The choice is yours. God bless you in Jesus' name. Amen!

CHAPTER THIRTY-TWO

CONTENTMENT

1 Timothy 6:6

> *"But godliness with contentment is great gain."*

To have great gain is a product of godliness and contentment. And contentment simply means satisfaction. Unfortunately, some people are hardly ever satisfied with what they have. When a person is not genuinely satisfied and happy with what they have, and they are not prepared to work hard to achieve a better status or condition, they are likely to open themselves up to jealousy, envy, greed, covetousness, and even stealing. Be happy, satisfied, and proud of what you have as a Christian.

These days, short people want to be tall, and tall people want to be short. Fat people want to be slim, and slim people want to be fat. It's better to be yourself. Psalm 139:14 says you are fearfully and wonderfully made. How about that? Be contented!

Some people are so consumed comparing themselves with other people. They wish they are what God has made somebody else. I just want to remind you that you are special. The Bible says in,

1 Peter 2:9

> *"But ye are a chosen generation, a royal priesthood, an holy nation, a peculiar people; that ye should shew forth the praises of him who hath called you out of darkness into his marvellous light:"*

Therefore, it's better not to make further comparisons. According to the scripture below, there is no wisdom in making comparisons between you and others. Set your own standards, and also use biblical standards for yourself, and don't compete unnecessarily with anyone. Run your own race in your own track looking onto Jesus the author and finisher of faith.

2 Corinthians10:12

> *"For we dare not make ourselves of the number, or compare ourselves with some that commend themselves: but they measuring themselves by themselves, and comparing themselves among themselves, are not wise."*

Many years ago, there was this couple in Nigeria, Mary and her husband Stephen, who were so poor that they could hardly afford three square meals a day, but they lived a life of total contentment. Their two children had no toys to play with and they hardly dressed well. But the couple worked hard as a team in their farm, harvesting yam, cassava, and vegetables. They truly loved one another, lived in peace, and trusted God as Christians for a better life. It was not long before the husband got a job in an oil Company and they moved from the village to the city living a modest much better life. When I saw Stephen, after he started his oil company job, I asked him about his new job and city life, he replied, "Not much difference because I have already learnt in my days of having almost nothing to be humble and contented in whatever situation I find myself." That's the true spirit of contentment.

I have been through periods of acute lack in my life with no proper job, and yet I lived in contentment not borrowing things from people, or complaining, or being envious of anyone. I simply trusted God to see me through the wilderness experience, and He did, providing me with manna all through until I got a proper job. Apostle Paul says in,

Philippians 4:11–12

> [11]*Not that I speak in respect of want: for I have learned, in whatsoever state I am, therewith to be content.*

> [12]*I know both how to be abased, and I know how to abound: everywhere and in all things I am instructed both to be full and to be hungry, both to abound and to suffer need.*

Being happy is not necessarily a result of a person having plenty stuff but it is simply a choice the person has made to be contented no matter the situation or circumstances. Apostle Paul says in verse 11 above that he has ***learned*** to be contented in whatever state he is. This means that we can learn to be contented. Learn it! Learn both how to be abased and how to abound. Whatever God has given you is the best. Love it! Cherish it! Be contented with it and you will see it appreciate in value more and more in Jesus' name. Amen!

CHAPTER THIRTY-THREE

YOU ARE NOT TOO OLD.

Stop telling yourself you are too old to do this or that, because you are definitely not. That's a lie of the devil. Age is just a number, and you can certainly put your mind to anything you desire and achieve it. Determine to prove your critics wrong, and that includes yourself. You have a lot of hidden talent you probably have not discovered about yourself. I never thought I could even write an article, but I write books now. God had deposited the writing anointing in me, and when the right time came, I started manifesting it. Similarly, there are certain talents you possess which you need to search inwardly and discover. There is a hidden hero in you that you need to unravel, and age can't stop it.

You are not too old to get a new job.
You are not too old to start your own business.
You are not too old to start your own ministry.
You are not too old to get married.
You are not too old to have children.
You are not too old to receive your healing.
You are not too old to start a degree course.
You are not too old to go into politics.
You are not too old to buy your own house.
You are not too old to buy a new car.
You are not too old to pass your driving test.
You are not too old to start gym and exercise.
You are not too old to...!!!!!!!

Stop putting yourself down, and bullying yourself, by saying, "I am too old to do this or that." A miracle is on the way for you so that you will know age is not a barrier for the Lord to favour you. Shout Amen!

Abraham received a calling for his ministry at the age of 75. He got his first child Isaac, at the age of 100, while Sarah was 90 after menopause. How about that? The fact that God did it for Abraham and Sarah is proof that He will do yours because God does not discriminate. He is not a racist either. Shout Hallelujah!

Perhaps you may say, "But the Abraham and Sarah's example is from the Bible." Now read the following life examples. Recently a 59-year-old woman I know gave birth to her first child after over 30 years of marriage. Nelson Mandela became South African President at the age of 75 after 27 years in prison. Ronald Reagan became American president at the age of 69. M. Buhari became the President of Nigeria for the second time at the age of 72. President Donald Trump of America came to power at the age of 70. Colonel Sanders, founder of KFC fried chicken started his business in his 60's. The list goes on and on. Check out your Guinness book of records today.

Just before I conclude this message, I want to add here that, apart from age, you should not consider any other factor as a limitation for you to make progress, and prosper. Never! God is more than able to lift you up. Keep trusting Him. Can I ask, "Are you too old?"

CHAPTER THIRTY-FOUR

FINISH THE TASK – JOHN 19:30

Finishing a task, business, or project is as important as starting it. And finishing is even more important because it's only when you finish that you start enjoying the benefits. As long as the task is half done, and uncompleted, you are not likely to enjoy the full benefits.

John 19:30

> *"When Jesus therefore had received the vinegar, he said, It is finished: and he bowed his head, and gave up the ghost."*

Jesus had one main task. And that was to die to save us. He accomplished that and said, "*It is finished*" just before He died. He completed the task. Apostle Paul is another person who fulfilled his purpose on earth before translating to be with the Lord. Read what he said in the scripture below.

2 Timothy 4:7

> *"I have fought a good fight, I have finished my course, I have kept the faith:"*

1 Kings 6:38-1 Kings 7:1

> [38]*And in the eleventh year, in the month Bul, which is the eighth month, was the house finished throughout all the parts thereof, and according to all the fashion of it. So was he seven years in building it.*
>
> [7:1]*But Solomon was building his own house thirteen years, and he finished all his house.*

King Solomon started building the Temple of the Lord and his own house and finished it as you can see from the above scriptures. As Christians, we also have to start and finish our tasks. Avoid unfinished business, and uncompleted projects. When you start reading an article or book, finish it. When you start a training course, finish it. When you start a business, finish it. When you start a project, finish it. When you start eating, finish it. When you start a journey, finish it. When you start... finish it!

Some people are in the habit of not finishing whatever they start. They get so excited about owning a four bedroom house with swimming pool, they buy it. And after a little while all the excitement is gone. They want another house. Some people are in the habit of starting a relationship and in no time all the excitement they had about this great lady or gentleman is gone. What has happened to this person they were madly in love with? Some are so excited about a job, business, car, church, school, country, etc. They get it, or get in and in no time all the excitement is gone.

It seems something is wrong here with this kind of trend. And my prayer is that the Most High God will help us all in Jesus' name. Tell yourself powerfully, "I will always start and finish my tasks by the grace of God in Jesus' name. Amen!"

CHAPTER THIRTY-FIVE

LET YOUR WORDS HEAL AND NOT WOUND – PROVERBS 12:18

Let your words heal and not stab and wound people.
Let your words comfort and console people.
Let your words edify and not discourage people.
Let your words refresh and bring hope to people.
Let your words strengthen and spur people to positive actions.
Let your words empower and bring people together in unity.
Let only words of wisdom proceed out of your gracious mouth.
Let not your words cause people to be offended and grieved.
Let your words not bring discord and scatter brethren and friends.
Let no filthy, corrupt, immoral, violent word proceed out of your blessed mouth.
Let no lying words proceed out of your mouth.
Let people count on your words as you speak true words of integrity.
Let your words minister life to people as you declare the gospel instead of gossiping.
Let your words be spoken in love.

Colossians 4:6

> *"Let your speech be always with grace, seasoned with salt, that ye may know how ye ought to answer every man."*

Proverbs 18:8

> *"The words of a talebearer are as wounds, and they go down into the innermost parts of the belly."*

Proverbs 12:18

> *"There is that speaketh like the piercings of a sword: but the tongue of the wise is health."*

Ephesians 4:29

> *"Let no corrupt communication proceed out of your mouth, but that which is good to the use of edifying, that it may minister grace unto the hearers."*

Remember that once words are spoken, you can't bring them back. Therefore, purpose today to think before you speak, and also speak edifying words.

PRAYER

Psalms 141:3

> *"Set a watch, O Lord, before my mouth; keep the door of my lips."*

Henceforth, Lord, I ask that you grant me the grace to only speak words of wisdom that will encourage, edify, comfort, and empower myself and people. "*Set a watch, O Lord, before my mouth; keep the door of my lips.*" Let no corrupt word proceed out of my blessed sanctified mouth in Jesus' name. Amen!

CHAPTER THIRTY-SIX

THE SPIRIT OF EXCELLENCE – DANIEL 6:3

Excellence has synonyms and some of them are – Awesome, fabulous, fantastic, high-class, marvelous, number one, splendid, superior, superb, and righteous. Our God is excellent, and we are created in His own image. Hence, everything about us ought to be excellent as well. The Bible says in:

Daniel 6:3

> *"Then this Daniel was preferred above the presidents and princes, because an excellent spirit was in him; and the king thought to set him over the whole realm."*

The above scripture tells us that Daniel was preferred above all the presidents and princes in the land of Babylon because an excellent spirit was in him. He did everything with a special touch of excellence. He's got the Midas touch.

As Christians, we are called into the ministry of excellence. How do you carry out your tasks at home and work? Is it with a special touch of excellence? Or is it done shabbily and in an awful pathetic manner? Do you realise that your good name is registered on every good work you do as a Christian? People will ask:

Who's the Caterer that cooked the food?
Who's the Drycleaner that cleaned the clothes?
Who's the Architect that designed the building?
Who's the Lawyer that handled the case?
Who's the choir Master in charge?

Who's the Teacher?
Who's the Nurse or Doctor that treated the patient?
The who is…? Is endless!

You will really get to understand how important it is to do excellent work when the result turns out to be excellent or bad. When the job done is excellent and people ask who did this work? You will confidently come out with smiles and full of joy for the whole world to see you and praise you. You have sown a good seed as per your name. A good name is better than gold and silver. But where will you hide your face when a bad job is done and people are asking, who did this awful job? Shame! The person will go into hiding. That will never be our portion in Jesus' name. Amen!

Colossians 3:23–24

> [23]*And whatsoever ye do, do it heartily, as to the Lord, and not unto men;*
>
> [24]*Knowing that of the Lord ye shall receive the reward of the inheritance: for ye serve the Lord Christ.*

As a Christian, purpose in your heart that henceforth, you will always do excellent work because we are to do whatever we do as unto the Lord as the above scripture declares. God also rewards us for the excellent work we do. To achieve excellence, we must be prepared to go the extra mile in whatever we do. Don't do a bad job because you are doing it voluntarily. Don't do a bad job because you are not well paid for the job. Remember, your name is on the work you do. Good or bad.

And Daniel was preferred to be at the helm of affairs in Babylon because he had an excellent spirit. When you do excellent things, you will be preferred to be in charge. You will be preferred to be favoured. Daniel was chosen to be a governor in various governments in Babylon as a foreigner. He was in King's Nebuchadnezzar, Belshazzar, and Darius governments as a Minister. Whao! That's what the spirit of excellence will do for a man. The spirit of excellence will always highlight you for favour, promotion, and blessings.

Excellence sells itself. When you have an excellent product or deliver excellent service, you don't need to spend much on advertising. All it takes for you to be known worldwide is for one person to use your product or service and go telling everyone about your excellent work. Excellence will promote and prosper you and your business.

Proverbs 22:29

> *"Seest thou a man diligent in his business? He shall stand before kings; he shall not stand before mean men."*

Henceforth, purpose to always do excellent work and you will be recognised and called to be honoured by kings. You will be given a national award and honour because of your outstanding excellent work. You are a royal. Do excellent work. God bless you in Jesus' name. Amen!

CHAPTER THIRTY-SEVEN

THERE IS ABUNDANCE OF EVERY GOOD THING.

We live in a world of abundance of good things including abundance of money. And I'm not joking! We have billionaires all around the world. All we need is a change of mentality, and begin to see abundance, and connect to the abundance of good things. The rule is, never see, think, or speak lack. Never! There is abundance of every good thing.

1. THE EARTH IS FULL OF RICHES

Psalms 104:24

> *"O Lord, how manifold are thy works! in wisdom hast thou made them all: the earth is full of thy riches."*

Whao! I'm so excited the above scripture says the earth is full of riches. Simply put, the earth is full of money, mineral resources, and other goodies. To be full means to be in a great measure, and abundance. Whao! I don't know about you. As for me, I see riches everywhere on earth and I enjoy it. Even if you don't physically have the riches now, the only way to partake of the riches on earth is for you to see, possess, and enjoy it by faith. Choose not to see lack, and never declare lack.

2. THE WHOLE EARTH IS FULL OF GOD'S GLORY.

Isaiah 6:3

> *"And one cried unto another, and said, Holy, holy, holy, is the Lord of hosts: the whole earth is full of his glory."*

Whao! I am getting more and more excited knowing that the whole earth is full of God's glory. Synonyms of the word glory include magnificence, splendour, prosperity, and wealth. And then the Bible says the whole earth is full of God's glory. Whao! What are you seeing on the earth? I don't know about you. As for me, I see the glory of God in everything and everywhere on earth! I am also enjoying the glory of God. As you see and declare it by faith, it will manifest.

3. JESUS HAS RELEASED ABUNDANT LIFE.

John 10:10

> *"The thief cometh not, but for to steal, and to kill, and to destroy: I am come that they might have life, and that they might have it more abundantly."*

I would like to believe everyone reading this book is a born again Christian because you must be born again to be entitled to claim or receive the above scripture. And even at that, Jesus is not forcing anybody to receive abundant life. That's why He said ***might...*** It's a choice! I don't know about you. As for me, I am born again, and I am enjoying abundant life that Jesus has freely given to me. Amen!

4. JESUS GAVE UP HIS RICHES FOR BORN AGAIN CHRISTIANS.

2 Corinthians 8:9

> *"For ye know the grace of our Lord Jesus Christ, that, though he was rich, yet for your sakes he became poor, that ye through his poverty might be rich."*

Whao! I love Jesus. He is a true and generous Daddy. He willed all His riches to born again Christians. I'm so excited about the inheritance. Jesus is the only one I know that gave up His riches for all Christians. Whao! I'm enjoying the riches Jesus gave me.

It's in abundance. Receive riches in abundance in Jesus' name. Note that Jesus couldn't have given up His riches for non-Christians because a Father's will normally go to the children.

5. GOD SAYS HE WILL GIVE US TREASURES OF DARKNESS, AND HIDDEN RICHES.

Isaiah 45:3

> *"And I will give thee the treasures of darkness, and hidden riches of secret places, that thou mayest know that I, the Lord, which call thee by thy name, am the God of Israel."*

Whao! Isn't God so kind? He says He will give us the treasures of darkness, and hidden riches of secret places. I am absolutely thrilled to know this. For those who can't see the abundance of good things upon the earth, God still says He will reveal them. I don't know about you. As for me, my spiritual eyes are open to see the treasures and hidden riches of secret places, and I am enjoying them abundantly.

I have just conducted a deliverance session from scarcity, lack, and poverty mentality to wealthy abundant mentality. Begin to walk with the consciousness of abundant wealthy mentality. And it shall be effectively made manifest.

CHAPTER THIRTY-EIGHT

ALWAYS BLESS YOUR FOOD AND DRINKS

One of the ways to ensure you remain healthy is to eat nutritious food. These days, food nutritionists and scientists discover different kinds of things about certain foods that we eat that makes it unsuitable for human consumption. It could be an acidic level of food, bacteria, side effects, or whatever. So what's the answer to fear or doubts about what we eat? Always bless your food and drinks!

Bless your food and drinks whether you know who cooked it or not, whether you are suspicious of the food or not, whether you are eating alone at home or eating with other people in a restaurant. Always bless your food and drinks! Eating nutritious blessed food will bring forth healing and help you remain healthy.

It doesn't have to be a long prayer. A simple prayer like this will do. "Father, I thank you for this food. I bless and sanctify it, and as I eat, let it nourish my body in Jesus' name. Amen!" And because you believe the simple prayer you made by faith in Jesus' name, every poison is automatically destroyed in Jesus' name. Amen! Don't be in a hurry and eat forgetting to pray, and then bless the food while it's in your belly. Exercise self-control no matter how tantalising the food may be and bless your food first. As you eat your food, also believe what Jesus said to us in ***Mark 16:18***, "*...And if they drink any deadly thing, it shall not hurt them...*" Remember you are what you eat. Always bless your food and drinks.

CHAPTER THIRTY-NINE

EXAMINE YOURSELF– 2 CORINTHIANS 13:5

A personal examination or assessment of your faith, and life in general is essential from time to time because it will enable you know whether you are making progress or not, as well as help you to review your plans. One of the reasons why people go astray is because they just keep on moving without actually having to pause and check whether they are still on track as they go towards their desired destination. Constant evaluation of your faith and plans will reveal any faulty area that needs to be corrected.

2 Corinthians 13:5

> *"Examine yourselves, whether ye be in the faith; prove your own selves. Know ye not your own selves, how that Jesus Christ is in you, except ye be reprobates?"*

Your Christian faith and life needs urgent examination if:

> You used to attend church services regularly, but don't attend anymore.
> You used to cast out demons, but you don't anymore.
> You used to read ten chapters of the Bible daily, but you don't read anymore.
> You used to pray daily, but you have stopped.
> You used to be a worker in the church but you stopped.
> You don't steal and defraud people before, but you do that now.

The Bible says in ***Proverbs 4:18*** that, *"But the path of the just is as the shining light, that shineth more and more unto the perfect day."*

This scripture states that as Christians, we are supposed to increase continually in glory. Hence, there should never arise an occasion where we will say, "I used to do this or that better before." If this happens, it's an indication that the person may have fallen out of faith, hence, they ought to honestly examine themselves.

The interesting thing about this examination is that you are in charge. You are to decide whether or not to examine yourself thoroughly. Nobody will cross examine you either. However, if a person doesn't examine themself properly, it will be to that person's detriment. Examine yourself whether you are still in faith. A genuine test of yourself that shows you are still in faith will help build up confidence and help you holistically.

2 Corinthians 13:5

> *"Examine yourselves, whether ye be in the faith; prove your own selves. Know ye not your own selves, how that Jesus Christ is in you, except ye be reprobates?"*

CHAPTER FORTY

CHARITY BEGINS AT HOME.

Start a demonstration of love with yourself, and then your immediate family, before outsiders. This is not selfishness, discrimination, or whatever anyone may want to call it. Even Jesus practiced this same principle. The Bible says in,

John 6:11

> *"And Jesus took the loaves; and when he had given thanks, he distributed to the disciples, and the disciples to them that were set down; and likewise of the fishes as much as they would."*

Jesus blessed the loaves, first took His own I suppose, and then distributed to His disciples, and the disciples after they have taken theirs, gave to the multitude. Can you see the sequence or order? Read below what happened in another situation in

Mark 7:27

> *"But Jesus said unto her, Let the children first be filled: for it is not meet to take the children's bread, and to cast it unto the dogs."*

We see again here that Jesus had a preference, and that is the children before the dogs. Of course, there will be special important instances when you may have to give preference to outsiders. For example, when you have to deal with vulnerable people, or really need to show compassion. But understand that you are not discriminating if you practice charity begins at home. Even if people call you names and perhaps criticise you, simply ignore them. After all, Jesus was also criticised by the Pharisees for all the good that He did. You can't please everybody. That's just a simple fact of life. God bless you. Amen!

CHAPTER FORTY-ONE

HARD TRUTH – TITHING

A woman left the church she was attending for another church because her Pastor preached that members should give tithe. When it comes to the issue of money, some Christians act as if to give of tithes and offerings is not biblical. Pastors didn't write the Bible. All they do is teach what the Word of God says.

The very first time this woman got to the new church, the new Pastor also preached on tithing and emphasised that some people leave one church and go to another because they don't want to hear the tithing message, and they don't want to give tithe. This was not a coincidence. It was the Spirit of God in operation. He will locate you anywhere you go to if you are disobedient.

What some people don't realise is that God is supreme and He is everywhere as in omnipresent God. Therefore, to change your church will not make you escape from God. He will catch up with you anywhere you go. ***Psalm 139:5-10,***

> 5*Thou hast beset me behind and before, and laid thine hand upon me.*
>
> 6*Such knowledge is too wonderful for me; it is high, I cannot attain unto it.*
>
> 7*Whither shall I go from thy spirit? or whither shall I flee from thy presence?*
>
> 8*If I ascend up into heaven, thou art there: if I make my bed in hell, behold, thou art there.*
>
> 9*If I take the wings of the morning, and dwell in the uttermost parts of the sea;*

> [10]*Even there shall thy hand lead me, and thy right hand shall hold me.*

To cut the long story short this woman was convicted and she went back to her former church and started tithing. Whao! This is good. This scenario does not apply only to tithing. It could be related to other areas of life. For example, fraud, prostitution, stealing, gossiping, laziness, pride, fornication, drug addiction etc. When a Pastor preaches the hard truth about what a person is not doing right, the spirit of obedience, humility, and repentance demands that the person should accept the truth, and repent and be more blessed. Obedience to the Word of God brings forth healing, while disobedience leads to bondage. When a person leaves the church because they heard the hard truth, that is rebellion, and it can lead to a person's destruction.

Proverbs 29:1

> *"He, that being often reproved hardeneth his neck, shall suddenly be destroyed, and that without remedy."*

There are people with stony heart and who lack conscience so to say. No matter how many times you preach the truth in the Word of God, they will remain hardened. Well, the above scripture says such people shall suddenly be destroyed and that without remedy.

> ***John 8:32,*** *"And ye shall know the truth, and the truth shall make you free."*

CHAPTER FORTY-TWO

THE BLAME GAME

A person is playing the blame game when he blames everything and everybody except himself when things go wrong. This is an unhealthy game to play. Take responsibility and be accountable when things are not right. This is integrity. Stop blaming your mother in law, boss, partner, witches, and wizards minus yourself for failures. Be accountable! Read below a scenario in the Bible showing blame game in operation.

Genesis 3:11–13

> [11]*And he said, Who told thee that thou wast naked? Hast thou eaten of the tree, whereof I commanded thee that thou shouldest not eat?*
>
> [12]*And the man said,The woman whom thou gavest to be with me, she gave me of the tree, and I did eat.*
>
> [13]*And the Lord God said unto the woman, What is this that thou hast done? And the woman said, The serpent beguiled me, and I did eat.*

The man blamed the woman, and the woman blamed the serpent. Who's at fault? Blaming everything and everybody except you when things go wrong is a sign of immaturity. And until you accept your responsibilities squarely, you may never grow up. Besides, the blame game will make you give away your power and energy thereby causing you to lose peace. When you stop the blame game, your healing will manifest.

CHAPTER FORTY-THREE

SERVE GOD FROM YOUR YOUTH– ECCLESIASTES 12:1

I heard the story of a very stingy man who saved everything until he retired at 65 to begin enjoying them. He deferred everything. Unfortunately, death struck shortly before his 65th birthday when he was due to retire. Now, is it bad to save? No! But you are meant to enjoy life all along until retirement and beyond, and not denying yourself the joy of celebrating life. What about deferring serving God until when you retire? Some people have it registered in their mentality that serving God should be in the evening of their life when they retire and are getting ready to translate to be with the Lord. What if death strikes before retirement? Well, let's see what the scripture has to say below.

Luke 12:20

> *"But God said unto him, Thou fool, this night thy soul shall be required of thee: then whose shall those things be, which thou hast provided?"*

The above scripture makes it clear that death can strike any time, therefore it is foolishness to keep saving or postponing things mainly for retirement. And the scripture below also tells us that Timothy had knowledge of the Bible right from his childhood days. Therefore, there is no excuse to defer reading the Bible as a child.

2 Timothy 3:15

> *"And that from a child thou hast known the holy scriptures, which are able to make thee wise unto salvation through faith which is in Christ Jesus."*

The scripture below also tells us that the Prophet Samuel ministered unto the Lord as a child. What excuse should adults have to serve God if Samuel started as a child?

1 Samuel 3:1

> *"And the child Samuel ministered unto the LORD before E'-li. And the Word of the LORD was precious in those days; there was no open vision."*

The scripture below further tells us that we should serve God from youth. Again, once a person dies, there will be no more opportunity to serve God.

Ecclesiastes 12:1

> *"Remember now thy Creator in the days of thy youth, while the evil days come not, nor the years draw nigh, when thou shalt say, I have no pleasure in them;"*

Psalms 6:5

> *"For in death there is no remembrance of thee: in the grave who shall give thee thanks?"*

Serving people is a sure way to moving up in life. Help vulnerable people whenever you can. Get involved in charity work. Give somebody help with your time. Our Lord Jesus Christ is a perfect role model for Christians. At the youthful age of twelve, He was already very active with the work of God to the extent that He had to stay in the temple with doctors both hearing them and asking them questions. His parents looked for Him everywhere and were in sorrow. This is the answer He gave them when they found Him in ***Luke 2:49***, *"And he said unto them, How is it that ye sought me? wist ye not that I must be about my Father's business?"*

Serving the Lord should not be done half-heartedly but wholeheartedly. ***Deuteronomy 10:12*** says, *"And now, Israel, what doth the LORD thy God require of thee, but to fear the LORD thy God, to walk in all his ways, and to love him, and to serve the LORD thy God with all thy heart and with all thy soul,"*

Our Lord Jesus Christ gave His whole life to serve God and humanity. Read below what He says about serving our fellow brethren in ***Mark 10:43-45***.

> 43 *But so shall it not be among you: but whosoever will be great among you, shall be your minister:*
>
> 44 *And whosoever of you will be the chiefest, shall be servant of all.*
>
> 45 *For even the Son of man came not to be ministered unto, but to minister, and to give his life a ransom for many.*

CHAPTER FORTY-FOUR

CHINESE BAMBOO

The Chinese bamboo is an amazing plant. I find the story about this plant fascinating and encouraging, and I hope you do too. Plant the Chinese bamboo today and expect it to germinate and start growing after a little while like other plants, but surprisingly nothing happens. Go ahead and water and fertilise it in the first year. Nothing noticeable happens. Absolutely Nothing! Do the same thing in the second, third, and fourth year, nothing happens. Absolutely nothing!

And suddenly in the fifth year, behold a miracle happens. The Chinese bamboo grows out and in just eight weeks it grows to amazing ninety feet. Incredible! What happened in the first four years? Obviously this plant has spent all those years growing its root downwards. The establishment of those invisible firm roots sustains the amazing growth as soon as it manifests.[5]

It's amazing how the things of nature turn out to be. Geologists have confirmed that mountains are sustained in depth by same equal rock in height above ground level. That is to say, if a mountain is 5,000 feet high, it is also 5,000 feet below as well.

The foundation of the building of a bungalow is nothing compared to the foundation of a Skyscraper. Engineers spend materials and time driving steel, iron, and concrete right down into the earth while constructing a Skyscraper and this takes a long time. But as soon as the foundation is completed, the rest part of the building progresses fast. And this in a way is even similar to the growth of the Chinese bamboo.

YOU COULD BE A CHINESE BAMBOO IN THE MAKING

Have you been labouring and making efforts regarding your career, business, and life generally, and it seems nothing good is manifesting? You have gone for training courses, invested more money, done adverts and promotions etc. (watering and fertilising) for your business, but nothing seems to be happening.

God is definitely working out things behind the scenes in your favour. It only seems nothing is happening, but an invisible transformation is certainly going on to bring you to the limelight. The heavens will surely open up to you and pour out to you so much blessing that you will not have room enough to receive it at the appointed time.

You've got to be patient because the roots growing downwards are certainly going to manifest fast upwards when the appointed time comes. God is building you up to be a formidable rock. Don't give up! Don't faint! Don't be discouraged! Just like the Chinese bamboo, you are manifesting good fruits for your labour speedily in Jesus' name. You are coming big, strong, and gloriously. And overtaking is also allowed. You will grow so fast, and overtake all those who took off before you in Jesus' name. Amen!

CHAPTER FORTY-FIVE

PREPARE TO BE MIGHTY

A lot people desire to be mighty in life and that is good indeed. But to be mighty does not just happen. Preparation comes before you become mighty. For example, when you prepare for an examination, you will pass. When you prepare for a sports event, you will win. When you prepare for your business, you will prosper. The scripture below tells of the secret of Jotham's success. Preparation! Bearing this in mind, we ought not to dabble into matters without adequate preparations. In order to excel in whatever we do, we must endeavour to prepare well.

2 Chronicles 27:6

> *"So Jotham became mighty, because he prepared his ways before the Lord his God."*

BENEFITS OF PREPARATIONS

Preparations will:

1. Make you pray, fast, and rely on God.
2. Make you research further.
3. Make you do enquiries about what you are about to do.
4. Make you to be detailed and thorough.
5. Reveal to you unexpected things you need to know and do.
6. Make you confident.

2 Chronicles 27:6

> *"So Jotham became mighty, because he prepared his ways before the Lord his God."*

Preparation will make you successful. You don't achieve success by being lucky. Quit cutting corners, scheming, and seeking for quick fix. To be the best in any field, you must be fully prepared. For example, to win an Olympic medal takes very serious preparations. The same goes for people who win awards for different things. You achieve such success through meaningful preparations. And it's important to mention here that having a good teacher, coach, or mentor will help your preparations. It may cost you money to hire somebody to help you prepare, but when you achieve your desired success you will also see that it is worth it.

CHAPTER FORTY-SIX

I SURRENDER ALL UNTO JESUS

A brother noticed that as they sang this popular hymn, *"I surrender all"* in church that a sister wasn't singing. And he asked her why she wasn't singing, and she said, "I am not singing because I am not ready to surrender all to Jesus and I don't deceive myself." That sounds terrible, doesn't it? Anyway this goes to show that it's not everybody you see in church is born again. Neither is everybody you see in church truly there to seek and worship God in spirit and in truth. Some are wolves in sheep clothing. The only unfortunate thing in this scenario about this sister is that to accept Jesus as your Lord and personal Saviour is not a decision to be postponed. It should be a ***now*** decision because the next minute may be too late.

I heard the story of a man who refused to receive salvation when they ministered to him. And in just a few hours, he was crossing a busy road and a car knocked him down and he died instantly and perhaps to end up in hell. Don't defer to receive salvation even for a second, because rapture can happen this very second.

The benefits of being a born again Christian is a lot. Let me give you a few. ***Firstly,*** it will help open the door way to heaven for you. ***Secondly,*** you will have a recreated spirit with the Holy Spirit dwelling in you. ***Thirdly***, you will be able to read the Bible and comprehend better because the Holy Spirit now dwells in you to teach you. ***Fourthly***, you will be able to speak in tongues and pray better. Isn't it wonderful to enjoy all these benefits absolutely free of charge?

Are you still considering whether to give your life to Jesus and surrender all to Him? It is better to have a rethink and do it now because the Bible says in ***2 Corinthians 6:2,***

> *"(For he saith, I have heard thee in a time accepted, and in the day of salvation have I succoured thee: behold, now is the accepted time; behold, now is the day of salvation.)"*

When is the accepted time of salvation? NOW!

As you accept to surrender all to Jesus now, please confess this: "I surrender my spirit, soul, body and everything I have to Jesus now. He is my Maker, and I accept Him as my personal Lord and Saviour. I believe wholeheartedly, and I confess with my mouth now that Jesus is Lord." Congratulations my friend. You are now a born again Christian. Go on and celebrate it.

CHAPTER FORTY-SEVEN

GENERATIONAL BLESSINGS

Please declare this powerfully: "I see, have, and enjoy generational blessings. I am blessed and highly favoured in Jesus' name. Amen!" Right from the beginning, the Bible says in,

Genesis 1:28

> *"And God blessed them, and God said unto them, Be fruitful, and multiply, and replenish the earth, and subdue it: and have dominion over the fish of the sea, and over the fowl of the air, and over every living thing that moveth upon the earth."*

As you can see from the above scripture, the blessing of the Lord was released unto man right from the onset in Genesis. The Bible says, "*And God blessed them...*" Therefore, have a positive mentality now as a Christian, and believe wholeheartedly that you are greatly blessed. Everything about you speaks the blessing of the Lord.

Ephesians 1:3

> *"Blessed be the God and Father of our Lord Jesus Christ, who hath blessed us with all spiritual blessings in heavenly places in Christ:"*

Whao! I am excited, and I believe you are too, knowing that you are blessed with all spiritual blessings. Hallelujah!

1 Peter 1:23

> *"Being born again, not of corruptible seed, but of incorruptible, by the word of God, which liveth and abideth for ever."*

2 Corinthians 5:17

> *"Therefore if any man be in Christ, he is a new creature: old things are passed away; behold, all things are become new."*

As a born again Christian, old things including so called 'generational curses' are passed away, and all things are become new. I reject, and destroy by Holy Ghost's fire every trace of generational curses. It will never be our portion in Jesus' name. Amen! Read below what God swore to do for Abraham and his seed of which you are one as a Christian.

Genesis 22:17-18

> 17*That in blessing I will bless thee, and in multiplying I will multiply thy seed as the stars of the heaven, and as the sand which is upon the sea shore; and thy seed shall possess the gate of his enemies;*
>
> 18*And in thy seed shall all the nations of the earth be blessed; because thou hast obeyed my voice.*

Galatians 3:29

> *"And if ye be Christ's, then are ye Abraham's seed, and heirs according to the promise."*

As a Christian, you belong to Jesus and the blessings of Abraham are all yours automatically.

2 Corinthians 8:9

> *"For ye know the grace of our Lord Jesus Christ, that, though he was rich, yet for your sakes he became poor, that ye through his poverty might be rich."*

My Lord Jesus gave up His riches and blessings and became poor so that we will be rich, wealthy, and exceedingly blessed. Hallelujah! Walk in this consciousness forever that you are indeed blessed. Henceforth, focus on generational blessings in Jesus' name. Amen!

CHAPTER FORTY-EIGHT

LET'S TALK ABOUT SEX

A brother in Christ once asked me the question below. I had to include it in this book because having a healthy romantic, loving, and sexual lifestyle will obviously serve as a healing balm to refresh the soul.

BROTHER: Is it right for a husband or wife to deny their partner sex because they have done something they don't like?

MY ANSWER: It is absolutely not right for anybody to deny their husband or wife sex just because they have done something they don't like. Sex is a very important aspect of a couple's marriage. Apart from the purpose of procreation, sex refreshes the soul. Therefore, have sex often, and if you've got the strength, do it daily. Many marriages are no longer exciting, and some others are as good as dead because romance, love, and constant sex have been excluded. Rekindle the fire in your marriage by engaging in serious romance, love, and sex. God created sex for married couples to enjoy. Therefore, enjoy it.

The Bible says in ***1 Corinthians 7:1-5***,

> [1]*Now concerning the things whereof ye wrote unto me: It is good for a man not to touch a woman.*
>
> [2]*Nevertheless, to avoid fornication, let every man have his own wife, and let every woman have her own husband.*
>
> [3]*Let the husband render unto the wife due benevolence: and likewise also the wife unto the husband.*
>
> [4]*The wife hath not power of her own body, but the husband: and likewise also the husband hath not power of his own body, but the wife.*

> [5]*Defraud ye not one the other, except it be with consent for a time, that ye may give yourselves to fasting and prayer; and come together again, that Satan tempt you not for your incontinency.*

Every married couple should look forward to a time to render due ***benevolence*** to their partner. And it's best to render it wholeheartedly, without reservations, being fully involved spirit, soul, and body in order to derive maximum satisfaction. It should be a time nothing else should matter to you in the world but you and the one you truly love. Verse 4 in the above scripture says you don't have full power over your own body anymore as your partner also has rights to it. Therefore, it's of no use denying your partner sex by making flimsy excuses. And the next verse reiterates this point by saying, "*Defraud ye not one the other, except it be with consent for a time, that ye may give yourselves to fasting and prayer; and come together again, that Satan tempt you not for your incontinency.*" The only time a couple should not have sex is a time of prayer and fasting, and that must also be with consent in agreement. It's not good to have sex during this period of fasting for purity and sanctification sake. Besides this, there must be absolute respect for one another's sexual feelings. You must not punish your partner by denying them sex.

Perhaps I should also mention here that when a woman is observing her menstrual cycle, it is not proper to have sex because of hygiene purpose and it is also biblical. See Leviticus 15:19. I know some couple may decide to use condoms but it's not hygienic and it's not biblical.

Ephesians 4:26

> *Be ye angry, and sin not: let not the sun go down upon your wrath:*

The above scripture advises us to settle our differences before night time. Be ready to say 'Sorry' and also forgive. Be angry but end your anger that same day before night time and be ready to have sex with your partner. No flimsy excuses!

CHAPTER FORTY-NINE

CAN A CHRISTIAN BE IN BONDAGE NEEDING DELIVERANCE?

The above was the question a sister in Christ asked me. I have given my personal answer to the question below, but it's definitely not exhaustive as you can also add your own contribution. Again, I have included this exciting question in this book because I believe once somebody is delivered from wrong mentality, they will be healed, and be free indeed and their soul will be refreshed.

MY ANSWER

YES and NO. The choice is yours to either believe or not to believe that you are bound or not bound as a Christian. I have chosen to sit on the fence here because it's a grey area. I believe it is primarily a mentality issue.

Proverbs 23:7

> *"For as he thinketh in his heart, so is he:.."*

What are your thoughts as a Christian? Do you think and believe that you are in bondage, suffer from generational curses, bewitched, under a spell, charmed, sick, and stagnated because of evil forces against you? If you think and believe this, it is likely to happen and be established. Jesus said to the two blind men who approached Him for healing in Matthew 9:29, be it done unto you according to your faith. This means positive or negative that you believe. It's now up to you to choose positive. Similarly, in ***Deuteronomy 30:19*** the Bible says, "*I call heaven and earth to record this day against you, that I have set before you life and* *death, blessing and cursing: therefore choose life, that both thou and thy seed may live:"* Make your choice.

Job 3:25

> *"For the thing which I greatly feared is come upon me, and that which I was afraid of is come unto me."*

From the above scripture, whatever any person fears, accepts, and believes is likely to happen and be established. Hence, it's better and healthy to believe only positive things. I would like to state here that witchcraft, charms, generational curses, stagnation and evil forces do exist. But as a Christian, it is better for you not to believe and accept that you are under any bondage and therefore you don't need any deliverance, because Jesus has set you free, and you are free indeed. Personally, I choose to believe that I am not under any kind of bondage, and will never be in the mighty name of Jesus. Amen!

YOU ARE NOT UNDER ANY CURSE AS A CHRISTIAN

2 Corinthians 5:17

> *"Therefore if any man be in Christ, he is a new creature: old things are passed away; behold, all things are become new."*

When you become a born again Christian, old things pass away, and you become a brand new creature. Hallelujah! How can a brand new creature be in bondage needing deliverance? The deliverance is from what? Will you conduct deliverance for a new born baby? Start thinking positively now as a Christian!

Ezekiel 18:20

> *"The soul that sinneth, it shall die. The son shall not bear the iniquity of the father, neither shall the father bear the iniquity of the son: the righteousness of the righteous shall be upon him, and the wickedness of the wicked shall be upon him."*

The soul that sinneth, it shall die. Period! You cannot be made to suffer for the iniquity of your fathers. That's what the above scripture says. So relax because you are not under any generational curse as a Christian.

Galatians 3:13

> *"Christ hath redeemed us from the curse of the law, being made a curse for us: for it is written, Cursed is every one that hangeth on a tree:"*

Christ has already redeemed every born again Christian including YOU if you are born again from the curse of the law. So you are not under any curse, and will never be as a Christian. You should be excited to know you are redeemed from every curse! Hallelujah! Simply believe the scriptures!

Colossians 1:13

> *"Who hath delivered us from the power of darkness, and hath translated us into the kingdom of his dear Son:"*

The above scripture says Christ hath (past tense) delivered every born again Christian from whatever bondage you may think of. So why do Christians still go about from one church and Pastor to another seeking and asking for deliverance?

As I round up this message, I would like to reiterate that as Christians, we must think and believe that we are not in bondage of any kind, because as a man thinks in his heart so is he. Declare this powerfully: "I am not in any bondage. I am not under any curse. I am free and free indeed in Jesus' name. Amen!"

CHAPTER FIFTY

PROSPERITY SCRIPTURES

Joshua 1:8

> *"This book of the law shall not depart out of thy mouth; but thou shalt meditate therein day and night, that thou mayest observe to do according to all that is written therein: for then thou shalt make thy way prosperous, and then thou shalt have good success."*

Job 36:11

> *"If they obey and serve him, they shall spend their days in prosperity, and their years in pleasures."*

Proverbs 28:13

> *"He that covereth his sins shall not prosper: but whoso confesseth and forsaketh them shall have mercy."*

Proverbs 10:4

> *"He becometh poor that dealeth with a slack hand: but the hand of the diligent maketh rich."*

Malachi 3:10

> *"Bring ye all the tithes into the storehouse, that there may be meat in mine house, and prove me now herewith, saith the LORD of hosts, if I will not open you the windows of heaven, and pour you out a blessing, that there shall not be room enough to receive it."*

Proverbs 3:9–10

[9]Honour the LORD with thy substance, and with the firstfruits of all thine increase:

[10]So shall thy barns be filled with plenty, and thy presses shall burst out with new wine.

Luke 6:38

"Give, and it shall be given unto you; good measure, pressed down, and shaken together, and running over, shall men give into your bosom. For with the same measure that ye mete withal it shall be measured to you again."

Psalm 1:1-3

[1]Blessed is the man that walketh not in the counsel of the ungodly, nor standeth in the way of sinners, nor sitteth in the seat of the scornful.

[2]But his delight is in the law of the Lord; and in his law doth he meditate day and night.

[3]And he shall be like a tree planted by the rivers of water, that bringeth forth his fruit in his season; his leaf also shall not wither; and whatsoever he doeth shall prosper.

3 John 2

"Beloved, I wish above all things that thou mayest proper and be in health, even as thy soul prospereth."

2 Chronicles 26:5

"And he sought God in the days of Zechariah, who had understanding in the visions of God: and as long as he sought the Lord, God made him to prosper."

2 Chronicles 20:20

> *"And they rose early in the morning, and went forth into the wilderness of Tekoa: and as they went forth, Jehoshaphat stood and said, 'Hear me, O Judah, and ye inhabitants of Jerusalem; Believe in the Lord your God, so shall ye be established; believe his prophets, so shall ye prosper."*

CHAPTER FIFTY-ONE

FAVOUR! FAVOUR!! FAVOUR!!!

Favour is a Spirit. The manifestation of the spirit of favour in a person or a peoples' life brings forth promotion, and fantastic results. Some of the synonyms of favour are grace, mercy, kindness, blessing, and love. You will find all these interchanged in the Bible depending on the verse and translation. Favour and grace share the same root word in Greek – ***Charis***. Grace is a free gift, but favour may be deserved or earned.

COMPLETE FAVOUR.

As a Christian, you need favour from both ***God*** and ***man***. That's complete favour. Read the scriptures below.

Luke 2:52

> *"And Jesus increased in wisdom and stature, and in favour with God and man."*

1 Samuel 2:26

> *"And the child Samuel grew on, and was in favour both with the LORD, and also with men."*

HOW TO ACTIVATE AND OBTAIN FAVOUR

As good, cherished, and wonderful as favour is, it may not just happen. You may need to do something before you obtain favour. I have discussed below some of the things you have to do to activate, and obtain favour.

1. GOOD UNDERSTANDING

Proverbs 13:15

> *"Good understanding giveth favour: but the way of transgressors is hard."*

You need good understanding of whatever you desire to be favoured in, for you to attract or obtain favour. For example, a Surgeon who desires a special award in the field of surgery needs to have good understanding by doing thorough research and work in the field of surgery. Once you do that, favour will appear and say, I am here for you. Obtain me. The Nobel prize for surgery with a lofty cash award will surface, and perhaps an international job with a fantastic pay. Whao! That's favour in operation. Don't fold your hands doing nothing waiting for favour to manifest. It may never happen.

2. BE GOOD

Proverbs 12:2

> *"A good man obtaineth favour of the LORD: but a man of wicked devices will he condemn."*

Proverbs 11:27

> *"He that diligently seeketh good procureth favour: but he that seeketh mischief, it shall come unto him."*

This point is pretty straightforward from the above two scriptures. Do you want to obtain favour of the Lord? If yes, be a good person. Logically, a bad person will not obtain favour of God. Choose this day to be good and obtain favour.

3. CONTINUOUS CONFESSION

Do you want to be favoured? Then you have to confess it day and night that you are blessed and highly favoured. Your confession starts now. What do you desire in life? Begin to confess it and call it forth, and it will manifest in due season. Be positive. Romans 4:17 says we should keep calling forth those things that be not as though they were. And Proverbs 18:21 says death and life are in the power of the tongue. And Numbers 14:28 says, as truly as I live, says the Lord, as you have spoken in my ears, so will I do to you. So let's go. Tell God all the goodies you want in line with the scriptures.

Let the weak say I am strong. Let the poor say I am rich. Let the redeemed of the Lord say so. The Lord is my shepherd, I shall not want. The Lord is perfecting all that concerns me. I am compassed with favour as with a shield in Jesus' name. Amen! This is how people who desire to be favoured talk.

4. WALK UPRIGHTLY

Psalms 84:11

> *"For the Lord God is a sun and shield: the Lord will give grace and glory: no good thing will he withhold from them that walk uprightly."*

When you walk uprightly as a Christian the above scripture says the Lord will not withhold good things or favour from you. Therefore, walk uprightly!

5. WISDOM

Proverbs 8:35

> *"For whoso findeth me findeth life, and shall obtain favour of the LORD."*

Walk in wisdom, and favour of the Lord will be yours forever.

6. EXCELLENCE

Daniel 6:3

> *"Then this Daniel was preferred above the presidents and princes, because an excellent spirit was in him; and the king thought to set him over the whole realm."*

Daniel had an excellent spirit. He had good training, and also did things in an excellent manner. That's why he was preferred, and picked by the king to be the head of government in Babylon even as a foreigner. That's favour!

Excellence sells itself. When you have excellent quality products and services, you will automatically attract customers. Sell to one person, and he will tell the whole world that your products and services are the best and people will come rushing for your products and services. Your customers will advertise you. Avoid mediocrity.

7. PREPARE YOURSELF TO BE FAVOURED

2 Chronicles 27:6

> *"So Jotham became mighty because he prepared his ways before the Lord his God."*

Preparation will put you in a position to be favoured. Jotham became mighty or favoured because he prepared himself perhaps through education and training, personal development and studies. 2 Timothy 2:15 - Study to show thyself approved by God. Good character, and networking with godly people of influence are things you can do that will help position you, and elevate you to be mighty or favoured.

8. GIVING

1Kings 3:3-5

> *3. And Solomon loved the Lord, walking in the statutes of David his father: only he sacrificed and burnt incense in high places.*
>
> *4. And the king went to Gibeon to sacrifice there; for that was the great high place: a thousand burnt offerings did Solomon offer upon that altar.*
>
> *5. In Gibeon the LORD appeared to Solomon in a dream by night: and God said, ask what I shall give thee.*

Solomon gave quality sacrifice and God appeared to him in verse 5 above, saying, "...*Ask what I shall give thee.*" This is favour! Give God your best and He will manifest to favour you.

9. KEEP SEEKING GOD

2 Chronicles 26:5

> *"And he sought God in the days of Zechariah, who had understanding in the visions of God: and as long as he sought the Lord, God made him to prosper."*

John 15:7

> *"If ye abide in me, and my words abide in you, ye shall ask what ye will, and it shall be done unto you."*

Keep on seeking God. Let His Word abide in you richly, and you shall continually enjoy His favour. Jesus says whatever you ask shall be done.

BENEFIT OF FAVOUR

The main benefit of favour is that it will promote you, and give you good speed in life to catch up with people ahead of you as well as overtake them. Favour will make you unique and special and also enable you enjoy life to the full.

THE PAIN OF FAVOUR

As good as favour is, note that you may need to step up prayers immediately you start receiving favour. Why? Envious and jealous people are likely to manifest displaying anger, and hatred. Use your powerful prayers to crush, and silence them, while trusting God to keep protecting you from all evil people.

TWO EXAMPLES OF FAVOURED PEOPLE

1. ABRAHAM

Genesis 24:1

> *"And Abraham was old, and well stricken in age: and the LORD had blessed Abraham in all things."*

2. VIRGIN MARY WAS FAVOURED TO BE THE MOTHER OF OUR LORD JESUS

Luke 1:28

> *"And the angel came in unto her, and said, Hail, thou that art highly favoured, the Lord is with thee: blessed art thou among women."*

The Lord bless, prosper, and favour you exceedingly in Jesus' name. Amen!

CHAPTER FIFTY-TWO

KEEP RENEWING YOUR MIND AS A CHRISTIAN – ROMANS 12:2

The mind is perhaps the most powerful tool a human being has. It is the human engine. It will perform well as long as you keep servicing it with the right stuff. When you upload the wrong stuff into the mind or leave it without renewal, it turns out bad. The mind is intangible, and it feeds our soul.

The Bible says we should keep on renewing our mind as Christians. The first reaction of some people would perhaps be that, my mind does not need to be renewed. But a simple proof that a person's mind needs continuous renewal is when a person is full of evil negative thoughts, speaks, and acts in an immoral, corrupt, violent, and arrogant manner. Another proof to show that the mind needs renewal is when negative, unpleasant things keep manifesting to a person.

The task of renewing the mind is a continuous one and it is for everyone including Bishop's and the Pope. How do we renew the mind? Studying and meditating on the Word of God are key ways for a Christian to renew the mind. The Bible says in,

Romans 12:2

> *"And be not conformed to this world: but be ye transformed by the renewing of your mind, that ye may prove what is that good, and acceptable, and perfect, will of God."*

We can also renew our mind by reading Christian books, and other meaningful books, magazines, and seeing and listening to positive edifying videos, and audios. Another way of renewing the mind is to carefully start getting rid of bad habits and sinful nature, and start developing new godly habits and character, through the power of the Holy Spirit.

Ephesians 4:22-24

> [22]*That ye put off concerning the former conversation the old man, which is corrupt according to the deceitful lusts;*
>
> [23] *And be renewed in the spirit of your mind;*
>
> [24]*And that ye put on the new man, which after God is created in righteousness and true holiness.*

The benefit of renewing the mind continually is that positive things will start manifesting in your life, you will be refreshed, full of joy, peace, and love of God, with a clear vision.

CHAPTER FIFTY-THREE

LOVE NOT THE WORLD – 1 JOHN 2:15–17

We are in the world as Christians, but our character and lifestyle should not be worldly. To live in a worldly way is to live life against the principles of the Word of God whereby everything goes. To be worldly is to walk in the flesh or to be carnal. It also has to do with being materialistic. There is nothing godly about being worldly and sadly such lifestyle is a path way to hell. On the other hand, to adopt a heavenly lifestyle is mainly about walking in the spirit. It entails studying the Word of God, and applying it in your life as a standard of living, and that indeed is a pathway to heaven. Read below what the scriptures says about being worldly and godly.

1 John 2:15-17

> [15]*Love not the world, neither the things that are in the world. If any man love the world, the love of the Father is not in him.*
>
> [16]*For all that is in the world, the lust of the flesh, and the lust of the eyes, and the pride of life, is not of the Father, but is of the world.*
>
> [17]*And the world passeth away, and the lust thereof: but he that doeth the will of God abideth for ever.*

Let's look at the following scriptures below making a comparison between carnality and spirituality. ***Romans 8:5–9***

> [5]*For they that are after the flesh do mind the things of the flesh; but they that are after the Spirit the things of the Spirit.*

> [6]*For to be carnally minded is death; but to be spiritually minded is life and peace.*
>
> [7]*Because the carnal mind is enmity against God: for it is not subject to the law of God, neither indeed can be.*
>
> [8]*So then they that are in the flesh cannot please God.*
>
> [9]*But ye are not in the flesh, but in the Spirit, if so be that the Spirit of God dwell in you. Now if any man have not the Spirit of Christ, he is none of his.*

This issue of loving the world is a serious one. Apostle Paul had to write to the church in Galatia saying in ***Galatians 6:8***,

> *"For he that soweth to his flesh shall of the flesh reap corruption; but he that soweth to the Spirit shall of the Spirit reap life everlasting."*

James also addressed the issue of a worldly lifestyle in his book. Look at how he put it in ***James 4:4***,

> *"Ye adulterers and adulteresses, know ye not that the friendship of the world is enmity with God? whosoever therefore will be a friend of the world is the enemy of God."*

Being worldly and materialistic will profit nothing. Jesus had to ask this question in ***Mark 8:36***, *"For what shall it profit a man, if he shall gain the whole world, and lose his own soul?"*

Apostle Paul gave us example of someone who loved the world. Demas was a Christian, and then loved the world and departed to Thessalonica. This is a typical example of backsliding in operation because the correct order should be that a worldly person received salvation and became a Christian, and not a Christian going back to his vomit to embrace worldly lifestyle again. What is backsliding? Backsliding is simply a backward or retrogressive movement which is dangerous and can never benefit anyone. A backsliding Christian is someone who is no longer serious with keeping up with his Christian lifestyle like reading the Bible, prayers, praise, worship, fellowship and abstinence from sin. Just imagine a human being that has his two eyes in front of his face now decides to be walking backwards without eyes. That is likely to lead to a crash after a little while because God created us to walk forwards. Always keep up with your spiritual lifestyle as a Christian.

2 Timothy 4:10

> *"For Demas hath forsaken me, having loved this present world, and is departed unto Thessalonica;..."*

Christians are heavenly kingdom citizens. Carry yourself with dignity in that manner and with that consciousness and you will continue to excel. Love not the world.

CHAPTER FIFTY-FOUR

HOW TO SET GOALS AND ACHIEVE THEM

Habakkuk 2:2-3

> [2]*And the Lord answered me, and said, write the vision, and make it plain upon tables, that he may run that readeth it.*
>
> [3]*For the vision is yet for an appointed time, but at the end it shall speak, and not lie: though it tarry, wait for it; because it will surely come, it will not tarry.*

From the above scripture, you can see that it's important for us to write our visions, dreams, or goals down. When you write it down, it's no longer a guess work, but it becomes concrete. The essence of setting goals is to give direction and guidance in order to achieve desired targets. Goals stop us from living life aimlessly.

A goal or a vision is simply a blueprint clearly set out in writing to be achieved for a specific period. What satellite navigation is to a car driver is what your goal is to you. It helps guide you to get to your desired destination. When you set out to build a house, you do a plan. Similarly, you also have to carefully design your life and set out to live out your dreams by putting one block upon another until your life appears as you have planned it to be. You can truly be the architect of your own life today by clearly writing your goal.

To live your life without a goal, is to live life without direction, or aimlessly. It's like playing football without goalpost; therefore, no target to aim at, and no goal will be scored. This sort of life is clearly a life of defeat, and failure. Thank God for this timely message as you take advantage of it and write your goals. It's important to note the following when you set goals.

THINGS TO NOTE ABOUT GOALS

1. Your goal must be specific.
2. You have to write your goal in a present continuous way. You can also write it in a declaration or affirmative way. For example, I am losing weight.
3. Your goal must be measurable in order to monitor progress. For example, my target is to lose weight from 100kg down to 80kg.
4. Your goal must be time bound or have a deadline. The weight loss goal should therefore be written as – My target is to lose weight from 100kg down to 80kg by the end of December this year.
5. You must work on your goals daily like a ritual. Continue to do even little things daily that will help you achieve your goals. Your brain responds to your goal as you work on it daily.
6. Your goal must be clear and precise.
7. You must have strategies, tactics, and a workable process for your goals. Therefore, develop a plan of action to follow through in order to achieve your desired goals.
8. You must be committed to your goals.
9. You must break away from habits that act as a barrier to achieving your goals, and develop the right new habits, beliefs, and values that will enable you to achieve your goals.
10. You must continually focus on positive things that will help you achieve your desired goal.
11. You must surround yourself with the right positive people who will support your goals rather than negative people who will tell you your goals are not achievable to discourage you.
12. Meditate, affirm, declare, and visualise your goals daily.
13. You must get rid of all fears, doubts, and unworthiness regarding you goals.[6]

As a guide, your goals can contain the following: Health targets, financial targets, family targets, spiritual targets, academic targets, and career targets. Set your goals today, and set yourself up on the path to greatness.

CHAPTER FIFTY-FIVE

YOU DON'T NEED MONEY TO START YOUR BUSINESS OR MINISTRY

When I first wrote this message a few years ago and posted it on my Facebook, a woman lashed out at me claiming that she totally disagreed with me. According to her then, she was looking for money to start her restaurant business and she needs money to rent a shop, furnish the shop, and buy various kinds of equipment. Meanwhile, this same message received a lot of likes and positive comments from wise people who understood and properly connected to the spirit of this message. I was not upset with her, but I immediately knew her level of mentality.

I am confidently saying it again - You don't need money to start your business, ministry, or whatever. Any time I see somebody who wants to start any kind of business and they keep saying they don't have the money to start, I see somebody who is clearly unprepared.

WHAT DO I NEED TO START MY BUSINESS?

You need the following things discussed below ***more*** than money to start your business.

1. BE PREPARED

2 Chronicles 27:6 says,

> *"So Jotham became mighty, because he prepared his ways before the LORD his God."*

Prepare fully regarding the business you want to start by equipping yourself with the necessary knowledge and wisdom. Fortify yourself with so much knowledge of how that business is done, by investigating it thoroughly. This means you must read books extensively, attend seminars, workshops, and have proper education and training. Once you are able to do this very well, it will raise your level of confidence very high and also inspire you because knowledge is power. This factor will really increase your value and enable you attract help and support you need to start your business.

2. BE READY TO START SMALL

This is where a lot of people miss it, including the woman that lashed out at me on Facebook for writing this message. If you don't have money to start your business in a big way, then start by doing it free or voluntarily for people. This is a powerful wisdom nugget I have just given to you. I have done this in my life and it worked, and I have seen it work in other people's lives. For example, when I wrote my first book, I didn't have any money. I had to borrow a computer from somebody, and later on I got an old rickety laptop to do my word processing. I had no money for publication but I didn't allow that to deter me. I went ahead to start with nothing and started taking a step of faith little by little and doors opened up for money to come in to publish it. Before I got my Job as a Church Administrator, I did it voluntarily for over one year before I was offered the job and put on the payroll. That's about starting small. I challenge you to start small now and see God divinely support you through destiny helpers He will send to you.

One of the problems people have today is that they are in a hurry to become big financially and in other areas. They are not patient. They are not willing to pay the price to be successful. They want to cut corners. They want to take short cuts and easy routes that may lead to a dead end. The Bible says in 1 Peter 5:10 that after you have suffered for a while, God will perfect, establish, strengthen, and settle you. Be willing to suffer for a while and pay the price for what you desire and God will show up for you in a big way.

I was in a barber shop one day to get my hair cut, and two men started talking about the owner of one nice African Restaurant in London. The proprietress is a Nigerian. One of the men knew this woman very well back in the 80's when she first started her business and confirmed that when she first started, she was cooking from ***home*** and giving out the food to people for ***free***. Yes, for free! She had no shop, but after a while she started charging money, and gradually it started growing, and then she opened a shop and her business started growing fast to become one of the most popular African Restaurant in London.

Most multinational big business you see today all started small. The problem with a lot of people is that they want to start big. So they go asking for loans from banks. And guess what usually happens? They mismanage the loan most of the time because they are inexperienced. But the truth remains that once you are fully prepared and you are ready to start small, God can stir you up to start, or as you start He will begin to send you destiny helpers who will support you. But you must start!

Job 8:7

> *"Though thy beginning was small, yet thy latter end should greatly increase."*

Zechariah 4:10

> *"For who hath despised the day of small things?..."*

God believes in, and supports humble small beginnings. He first created Adam, and then added Eve. Today the world population is over six billion. Jesus started by calling His disciples one by one until He got twelve Apostles and eventually got several disciples. Start small. Don't despise the days of small things.

3. TAKE A STEP OF FAITH

Faith is now according to Hebrews 11:1. You must be prepared to leave the state of inertia. When? NOW! As long as you don't make any move, nothing will happen.

James 4:8

> *"Draw nigh to God, and he will draw nigh to you..."*

From the above scripture, who will make the first move? YOU! Yes it's YOU! As you do, God will step in to support your business. You will start attracting the right help and support you need. The forces of nature and the universe have a mysterious way of helping those who take a step of faith in the right direction. You will just find that the building blocks will be added one upon another gradually until your business is established and starts expanding fast.

4. SUPPORT ANOTHER BUSINESS

Luke 16:12

> *"And if ye have not been faithful in that which is another man's, who shall give you that which is your own?"*

If you are finding it hard to start, go ahead, voluntarily and faithfully begin to support another business owner as the scripture above says. As you do so, Jesus will make a way for you to have yours. Supporting another business owner will enable you gain more experience and training as well as exposing you to the right network, to be divinely connected to destiny helpers. The problem a lot of people have is that they want to be wealthy overnight. They don't want to know that before they become wealthy, they have to pay the price. Therefore to work for free or voluntarily for another man is too difficult for them to comprehend and do. Just follow Jesus' advice in the above scripture.

5. INTEGRITY

Integrity means honesty and uprightness. Integrity is an asset. Can you be trusted by people? If yes, they will even give you goods on credit to sell and later you will return their money after you have sold the goods and made your profit. I know a few people who started and built big businesses like this. They can even give you some good connections to important people because they know you are honest and therefore will not let them down. People are more likely to give you any kind of support you ask for all because you have integrity. That's why the Bible says in,

Proverbs 22:1

> *"A good name is rather to be chosen than great riches, and loving favour rather than silver and gold."*

Can your name be mentioned and people will not shout and say, "Ah! Please don't do business with that guy. He will dupe you if you try it. He is a fraudster." If people say this about you, then you don't have integrity and you will find it hard to get help. That person needs to work on their character and change for good first.

After my friend's son Martin graduated from university as a Biochemist in Nigeria, he couldn't get a job for over two years, and my friend said I should pray for his son to get a job. After praying, I counseled Martin to start offering a free service teaching secondary school students who want to sit for their GCE and JAMB examinations. He heeded to my advice. He immediately got together about ten teenagers and started teaching them Biology and Chemistry free of charge. He only did that for six months and got a teaching job in a private secondary school in Lagos. Guess what? It was the boys who he was teaching for free who strongly recommended him for this teaching job. They told the principal of the school that Martin is the best Biology and Chemistry teacher in the world. The Principal was excited and hired him.

When my Facebook friend Judith couldn't get a Care Assistant job after her training in Jamaica, she called me a few times to pray for her. And after prayers one day, I suggested to her that she should find some elderly people in her neighbourhood and start rendering free care service to them, she heeded my advice and she immediately started helping a few elderly people to do their shopping, cook, clean their houses, clean and iron their clothes free of charge. Guess again what happened? It was one of the elderly people she was caring for who linked her up to get a well-paid Care Assistant job in a reputable company after eight months voluntary service. She called me to share her testimony and thank me for giving her the advice.

What I am sharing here applies also in setting up a ministry, charity, or other organisations. Some Ministers of God want to open a church and start it big, fully furnished with air condition and all amenities. Therefore, they go seeking a loan from the bank. My friend, start the church from your living room apartment and over time the church will grow and you will get a bigger place of worship. Start small.

What I am writing here is what I have proven in my own life and have also seen it happen to people provided the business or project is of God. Not a fraudulent business. I hope I have been able to convince somebody here that you don't need money to start your business or ministry.

CHAPTER FIFTY-SIX

WHAT THE BIBLE SAYS ABOUT LIES & LIARS

As you read this book you may ask, "What has lies and liars got to do with a healing book?" Well, lies has a lot to do with healing because most people find themselves in serious bondage basically because of their lies, and when they stop lying healing will manifest and they will be free indeed.

WHAT IS A LIE?

A lie is an account or statement of what is not true. A lie is also an exaggeration of what actually happened. A lie can be deliberate when it is meant for evil to tarnish the image of another or to obtain something through falsehood. A lie may genuinely not be deliberate, and this happens when somebody makes a statement without having adequate information about the matter.

A lie is a lie. There is no small or big lie in the eyes of God. For example, as simple as when somebody says, "I will call you back on the phone, or see you later," and does not do it, it amounts to a lie. To make a promise and not keep it or not keep it at the right time is also a lie.

Lies are associated with the devil according to,

John 8:44

> *"Ye are of your father the devil, and the lusts of your father ye will do. He was a murderer from the beginning, and abode not in the truth, because there is no truth in him. When he speaketh a lie, he speaketh of his own: for he is a liar, and the father of it."*

Therefore, from this scripture we can conclude that the devil is using anyone lying.

THE DANGER OF LYING

There is a saying that goes like this, "Liars must have good memory." Unfortunately, Liars are good at changing the story forgetting what they said before thereby causing offence and constituting a nuisance. But when you tell the truth, you don't have to worry about changing your story because you told the truth.

Another interesting thing about lies is that when somebody lies once, they are likely to lie again and again, and it will soon become a lifestyle. Therefore, it's better not to lie even once. You don't need to take an oath to tell the truth. Just let your yea be yea, and nay be nay. Again, when somebody lies, they belittle themselves. Lying is a dishonest act, therefore, anyone who lies lacks integrity and the lie belittles that person.

The Bible says in,

John 8:32

> *"And ye shall know the truth, and the truth shall make you free."*

Logically, if the truth will make people free, then lies will put people in bondage. For example, somebody is well but, calls his employer to declare he is sick just because he wants to be off from work. Satan will now ensure that the person becomes sick if not in the body, then in some other ways. It's time to outsmart the devil and give up lying.

Lying is so terrible and that's why the Bible also has scriptures covering the subject. Let's look at some of the scriptures below.

Proverbs 19:5

> *"A false witness shall not be unpunished, and he that speaketh lies shall not escape."*

Proverbs 19:9

> *"A false witness shall not be unpunished, and he that speaketh lies shall perish."*

Psalms 31:18

> *"Let the lying lips be put to silence; which speak grievous things proudly and contemptuously against the righteous."*

Proverbs 12:19

> *"The lip of truth shall be established for ever: but a lying tongue is but for a moment."*

Revelation 21:8

> *"But the fearful, and unbelieving, and the abominable, and murderers, and whoremongers, and sorcerers, and idolaters, and all liars, shall have their part in the lake which burneth with fire and brimstone: which is the second death."*

To lie is unhealthy because it causes others to be offended, makes people lose confidence in you, reduces your value and respect. Lying can also make you lose valuable friends and customers because they don't trust your words. And most importantly, all liars will end up in the lake of fire – Read Rev. 21:8 above again. The lake of fire is not a place to be. Potiphar's wife probably ended up there for lying that Joseph attempted to rape her, and innocent Joseph was thrown into prison.

As Christians we must purpose to avoid all small and big lies. Determine to come clean, and avoid falsehood in our life endeavours because whatever anyone gets through lies, and deceit, they are likely to lose. It's a question of time.

CHAPTER FIFTY-SEVEN

POSITIVE INTERPRETATION

No event, situation, or circumstance has meaning except for the meaning you give or how you view and process it. The meaning you give can either be,

Good or bad
Positive or negative
Optimistic or pessimistic
Advantageous or disadvantageous

When my friend Joseph Elliot lost his job as a Financial Analyst in one of London's Merchant Banks, he was gutted and felt like that was the end of the world. However, he took a new approach and began to see the positive side of things and started feeling better. No matter the intensity of the storm that may come against a person, I say be strong and of good courage because it will come and go. God has promised that He will never leave us, nor forsake us. Therefore things may seem to be very bad, but remember that God is a specialist in turning around situations that seem so terrible into victories. Anyway, Joseph Elliot started his online distributorship business, which started booming and he even became an employer of labour. This wouldn't have happened if he didn't lose his job. When one door closes many more, better doors will definitely open up. That's how people who make positive interpretation think. What you call a mess, shame, disappointment, or failure is what God will use to promote you. Just be calm and trust Him.

It's a matter of choice how we interpret life events, situations, and circumstances. Determine to interpret life events and situations positively and all things, no matter how bad it may seem will work together for your good. God is a master planner and He has predestined things about us right from the foundations of the world. He knows our destinations in life and He has the plans to get us there, but He doesn't reveal the plans to us. If He reveals the plans to us, we may not want to embark on the journey to get to the destination. As we set out on our journey following our plans or His plans to get to the destination, we are likely to experience stumbling blocks along the way and these may be ugly, bad, or good and they all serve as training to get us to the destination. The good news is that eventually God will put together all we have been through, ugly, bad, or good to work together for our good to get us to His original destination for us. Therefore, you don't need to worry too much about those mistakes you made in your life's journey, which seems terrible because in the end they will all play out in your favour as God will use all things to work for your own good.

Romans 8:28

> *"And we know that all things work together for good to them that love God, to them who are the called according to his purpose."*

All things will indeed work together for our good when we also have the right mentality and attitude, being optimistic and interpreting events and situations positively to our own advantage.

While we discuss positive interpretations, I would like to also briefly touch on ***hermeneutics***, which essentially deals with scriptural interpretations. Correct interpretation and application of scriptures in our life will yield good results. Correct interpretation of scriptures also depends on proper understanding of the Word of God.

Therefore it is important that you are a ***born again Christian*** in order to understand scriptures. Apostle Paul made it clear in **1 *Corinthians* 2:14** of ***The Living Bible*** that, *"The man who isn't a Christian can't understand and can't accept these thoughts from God, which the Holy Spirit teaches us. They sound foolish to him because only those who have the Holy Spirit within them* *can understand what the Holy Spirit means. Others can't just take it in."*

It is only when you understand a scripture well that you can correctly apply it in your life. I have seen some people including corrupt minded Christians make a mockery of the Word of God by twisting the truth in the Word of God and applying the scripture in a manner to suite their selfish evil ways. Remember that it's only when we correctly interpret and apply scriptures that it will yield good results.

2 Timothy 2:15 says,

> *"Study to shew thyself approved unto God, a workman that needeth not to be ashamed, rightly dividing the word of truth."*

God approves those who study because they acquire knowledge and wisdom of God. We need to study in order to be able to, "rightly divide the word of truth." To rightly analyse, and interpret the Word of God, comparing scriptures with scriptures requires skill, and you acquire such skill from studying. Let us have a look at what the Berea Christians did.

Acts 17:10-11 says,

> *10 And the brethren immediately sent away Paul and Silas by night unto Berea: who coming thither went into the synagogue of the Jews.*
>
> *11 These were more noble than those in Thessalonica, in that they received the word with all readiness of mind, and searched the scriptures daily, whether those things were so.*

Search the scriptures daily and grow in your understanding, interpretation, and application of scriptures.

CHAPTER FIFTY-EIGHT

HOW TO BE LED BY GOD

One of the challenges Christians face is the ability to perceive, hear, understand, and know distinctively the leading of God. So how does God lead Christians? The leading of God in all that we do is very essential in order not to go astray. Let us look at a few ways below.

1. THE BIBLE

The most authentic way to be led as a Christian is with the Bible. And as a matter of fact, the other ways we can be led by God should also point us to what the Bible says as a confirmation. As you study the Bible, have an open heart, and be expectant that you will receive a revelation that will be fired up in your spirit inspiring and leading you on what to do.

Job 36:11

> *"If they obey and serve him, they shall spend their days in prosperity, and their years in pleasures."*

Any time you are not very sure what to do about a situation, and you are determined to move forward, simply boldly hold on to appropriate scriptures and confidently act on them by faith. And as you do so, that is you being led by God. I think it is better to keep acting on the Word of God by faith, than remaining static and claiming you don't have any idea what to do. Obedience to the Word of God does yield positive results.

2. VISIONS

Vision is a supernatural revelation of things from God to a person mainly while awake. It usually comes like a flash, or as in seeing pictures like a person watching television, or maybe when in a trance. And because it is a revelation from God, the vision is surely bound to happen. And a careful analysis of the vision is likely to have a bearing with what the Bible says. Or you can ask God to give you a scriptural reference concerning the vision He has shown to you.

In ***Acts 10:9-19*** Apostle Peter was in a trance and God showed him a vision. This is a good example of a vision from God.

3. DREAMS

Some people confuse dreams with visions but they are not exactly the same. Essentially, a dream is supernatural revelation from God to a person while the person is sleeping. A dream is also supposed to tie up with scriptures. Just ask God the meaning.

1 Kings 3:5

> *"In Gibeon the Lord appeared to Solomon in a dream by night: and God said, Ask what I shall give thee."*

The above scripture is a good example of a person having a dream at night while sleeping.

Joel 2:28

> *"And it shall come to pass afterward, that I will pour out my spirit upon all flesh and your sons and your daughters shall prophesy, your old men shall dream dreams, your young men shall see visions:"*

If your dream does not have a bearing with the scriptures in some way, then it's an indication you may have had a horrible nightmare perhaps because you spent a great deal of the day time feeding yourself with junk, perhaps watching immoral, violent, or some scary films, or engaged in terrible activities, and when you went to sleep you recalled your daytime experiences while asleep. Nightmare! This is not of God.

Be careful when interpreting dreams. Once a dream is bad, quickly reject it and pray against it happening because it is likely to be from the devil. But when a dream is positive, quickly claim and accept it, and even pray for the speedy manifestation.

4. RHEMA OR SPOKEN WORD OF GOD

Logos refer to the written word of God or Bible, while Rhema refers to the spoken word of God. As a Christian, you are entitled to hear God. Read what Jesus said in,

John 10:27

> *"My sheep hear my voice, and I know them, and they follow me:"*

From the above scripture, Christians ought to hear the voice of God. But rebels cannot hear God because they are not His sheep. A rebel is a disobedient person. God can also speak to a disobedient person to warn him to refrain from his evil ways.

Isaiah 30:21

> *"And thine ears shall hear a word behind thee, saying, This is the way, walk ye in it, when ye turn to the right hand, and when ye turn to the left."*

1 Samuel 3:10

> *"And the Lord came, and stood, and called as at other times, Samuel, Samuel. Then Samuel answered, Speak; for thy servant heareth."*

1 Samuel 3:1-10 is example of a passage in the Bible where we see God calling Samuel again and again. That's an example of God's spoken word to a person.

5. THE HOLY GHOST SPEAKS

The Holy Spirit can speak to lead a Christian. The Holy Spirit can speak in the form of you perceiving or discerning something by the Holy Spirit, or hearing a small still voice, or you hearing loudly. Let's look at some scriptures below.

Acts 13:2

> *"As they ministered to the Lord, and fasted, the Holy Ghost said, 'Separate me Barnabas and Saul for the work whereunto I have called them'."*

Acts 21:11

> *"And when he was come unto us, he took Paul's girdle, and bound his own hands and feet, and said, Thus saith the Holy Ghost, So shall the Jews at Jerusalem bind the man that owneth this girdle, and shall deliver him into the hands of the Gentiles."*

Revelation 2:7

> *"He that hath an ear, let him hear what the Spirit saith unto the churches; To him that overcometh will I give to eat of the tree of life, which is in the midst of the paradise of God."*

The above scriptures confirm that the Holy Spirit speaks. Listen and you will hear Him speak. Looking at Acts 13:2 above again, it says the Holy Ghost spoke as they ministered to the Lord, and fasted. This is an indication that your spiritual exercise as a Christian which includes fasting, prayers, studying the Bible, praise, worship and abstinence from sin can activate the Holy Spirit to speak.

6. PROPHET OF GOD

God can send His Prophet or any other person to talk to you about something that will serve as a leading to you. When King David messed up with Bathsheba, God sent Prophet Nathan to him. That's how God can send a Prophet to you regarding a matter.

2 Samuel 12:7

> *"And Nathan said to David, Thou art the man. Thus saith the Lord God of Israel, I anointed thee king over Israel, and I delivered thee out of the hand of Saul;"*

7. ANGEL OF THE LORD

God can send His angel to you to speak to you in order to lead you concerning any issue. Angels are spirit beings, but may appear in the form of human beings. Angel Michael and Gabriel are examples in the Bible.

Judges 13:3

> *"And the angel of the Lord appeared unto the woman, and said unto her, Behold now, thou art barren, and bearest not: but thou shalt conceive, and bear a son."*

Luke 1:26-28

> 26*And in the sixth month the angel Gabriel was sent from God unto a city of Galilee, named Nazareth,*
>
> 27*To a virgin espoused to a man whose name was Joseph, of the house of David; and the virgin's name was Mary.*
>
> 28*And the angel came in unto her, and said, Hail, thou that art highly favoured, the Lord is with thee: blessed art thou among women.*

I haven't seen an angel before; therefore I am unable to give a physical description of an angel here. Perhaps when somebody visits and speaks to you and then disappears, it's an indication he may be an angel. Angels certainly exist. And the above scripture confirms that.

8. THE PEACE OF GOD

When you have the peace of God regarding a matter, it's an indication of the leading of God to go ahead. But when you are restless, and having no peace, it's an indication not to proceed.

Isaiah 55:12

> *"For ye shall go out with joy, and be led forth with peace: the mountains and the hills shall break forth before you into singing, and all the trees of the field shall clap their hands."*

Apart from the points mentioned above, a Christian can be led through some other ways, but I have discussed some of them above. My prayer for you is that you will never go astray. You will continually receive the right leading of God in all that you do in Jesus' name. Amen!

CHAPTER FIFTY-NINE

REASONS WHY YOU SHOULD BE IN CHURCH

You may ask again saying, "What has going to church got to do with healing?" Well, going to church has a lot to do with healing and you will see that from the points discussed below. For example, the church is a miracle centre and loads of people receive their healing there. I have seen people who claim to be Christians who don't go to church. They have ready defence why they don't have to be in church. For example, they will say things like:

Church is in the heart.
They ask for too much money in church.
The church is too far.
I'm facing some trials at the moment.
I'm too busy with my job or business.
I don't have the time for church.
I don't like church folks etc.

My friend, whatever your reason may be, God is saying today you should prayerfully choose a local church where you should worship. No more excuses! You never know, you may have to be in church to receive the healing you desire. Now let's look at the reasons why you should be in church.

1. IT IS THE COMMANDMENT OF GOD

Exodus 20:8

> *"Remember the Sabbath day, to keep it holy."*

2. JESUS OUR ROLE MODEL WENT TO CHURCH

Luke 2:46

> *"And it came to pass, that after three days they found him in the temple, sitting in the midst of the doctors, both hearing them, and asking them questions."*

Luke 4:16

> *"And he came to Nazareth, where he had been brought up: and, as his custom was, he went into the synagogue on the sabbath day, and stood up for to read."*

3. JESUS LOVED THE CHURCH. SO, DON'T HATE THE CHURCH

Ephesians 5:25

> *"Husbands, love your wives, even as Christ also loved the church, and gave himself for it;"*

4. KING DAVID SAYS HE WAS GLAD TO BE IN CHURCH. WHAT ABOUT YOU?

Psalms 122:1

> 1 *"I was glad when they said unto me, Let us go into the house of the Lord."*

5. THE CHURCH IS A LEARNING CENTRE

The scriptures above in Luke 2:46 and 4:16 tells us that Jesus was in church hearing and asking questions and also read the Bible. I know many people who joined a church and became a worker and learned skills which they now use. For example, some music celebrities started in the church choir. You can also join the church technical department and learn audio and video recording. Joining the publications department will give you opportunity to learn and develop your writing and printing skills, or you can join any other department and learn new things.

Acts 5:42

> *"And daily in the temple, and in every house, they ceased not to teach and preach Jesus Christ."*

6. THE CHURCH IS A PLACE OF FELLOWSHIP

The scripture below encourages Christians to fellowship together. Note that there are certain challenges you may not be able to tackle alone. Therefore, you need corporate anointing with other believers in order to end such challenges.

Hebrews 10:25

> *"Not forsaking the assembling of ourselves together, as the manner of some is; but exhorting one another: and so much the more, as ye see the day approaching."*

7. SOCIAL CENTRE

There are many social activities, and associations you can join and benefit from in the church. In Acts 6:1–4 members were served food.

8. MIRACLE CENTRE

Different miracles, healings, and deliverances happen in church. So join a church and receive yours. For example, in Luke 13:12-14, the woman with the spirit of infirmity was healed in the synagogue. Apart from biblical examples, I have seen and heard a lot of people share their testimony in church how God healed them, maybe when the preaching was going on, or when they used the anointing oil, had Holy Communion, hands laid on them, they used their blessed handkerchief or whatever. God bless you abundantly in Jesus' name as you resume Church.

CHAPTER SIXTY

BEWARE OF JUDAS

Love is a powerful tool to heal, unite, and bond people, but it seems the Judas' of this world are hardened, no matter how much love you show them. Each time I ponder on the fact that Jesus Christ even showed Judas agape love, and he still betrayed Him, it makes me puzzle. If Jesus showed agape unconditional love to Judas and he still betrayed Him, why should I complain when people let me down after showing them plenty of love? Nothing can be as painful as having the very person you showed love turn around and stab and wound you in a wicked betrayal. That's why you have to be on your guard and shield yourself from Judas betraying you. Judas may strike at the beginning of the relationship, or after a seemingly well-bonded relationship has been built up. Whatever the case may be, open your eyes, and discern things.

This message is very important because it is about guarding yourself in the first place from being hurt so that there will be no need for healing. Many people have been emotionally wounded today by Judas who they loved. Judas could be anyone including your closest loved ones. After all Judas was one of Jesus' twelve Apostles. They were very close. He was Jesus' treasurer. To avoid being hurt and be in pain, you must avoid Judas. Be on guard against him.

Romans 16:17

> *"Now I beseech you, brethren, mark them which cause divisions and offences contrary to the doctrine which ye have learned; and avoid them."*

Luke 22:3–6

> [3]*Then entered Satan into Judas surnamed Iscariot, being of the number of the twelve.*

> [4]*And he went his way, and communed with the chief priests and captains, how he might betray him unto them.*
>
> [5]*And they were glad, and covenanted to give him money.*
>
> [6]*And he promised, and sought opportunity to betray him unto them in the absence of the multitude.*

Jesus Christ of Nazareth had twelve Apostles, and one of them was Judas. Before Judas betrayed Jesus, he was a good man. That's why Jesus chose him to work with Him. "*Then entered Satan into Judas surnamed Iscariot...*" Whao! To start with, the fact that Judas was an Apostle shows there is absolutely no one Satan cannot enter. Satan can enter men and women of God, family members, friends, strangers, etc. Don't express shock at this because the Bible even says in ***Matthew 10:36***, "*And a man's foes shall be they of his own household.*" Note that it was after Satan entered Judas that he set out to betray Jesus.

HOW DOES SATAN ENTER PEOPLE?

Satan can enter a person through greed for money. See Luke 22:5 above. It can also enter through strife, anger, bitterness, immorality, pride, wickedness, and sin. Through what people see, hear, think, and talk about. Guard your heart with all diligence.

We must be prepared to work on our character to be good Christians, and not make sin a lifestyle. We must not yield or co-operate with Satan, and allow him to enter us. Be on guard! ***Ephesians 4:27*** says, "*Neither give place to the devil.*" Open your spiritual eyes and quickly spot the appearance of Judas, and deal with him decisively. Greed for money is one of the traits. See ***Luke 22:5*** above. Allow the Holy Spirit to guide you in all you do. As you do this, he will reveal Judas and his betrayal intentions to you quickly.

Finally, the Bible declared that Judas returned the thirty pieces of silver he collected to betray Jesus, and went and hanged himself. What a way for a betrayer to die! My prayer today is that all those who betray us will hang themselves and die even as Judas did in Jesus' name. Amen!

CHAPTER SIXTY-ONE

DOING BUSINESS IN A GODLY WAY

When people don't do their business in a godly way, they are likely to get into trouble, experience challenges, or business failure, which can effectively lead to emotional pain needing healing. Prevention is better than cure. Therefore, avoid cutting corners, scheming, and greed in business. Adhere to government standards, policies, and legislation.

Doing your business in a godly way means that you will put God first, and above your business. The fear of the Lord is the beginning of wisdom. He gave you power to make wealth. Honour Him. Apply the following principles and do your business in a godly way.

1. MAKE THE WORD OF GOD YOUR COMPANION.

To be a successful business person, you have to make the Word of God your companion.

Joshua 1:8

> *"This book of the law shall not depart out of thy mouth; but thou shalt meditate therein day and night, that thou mayest observe to do according to all that is written therein: for then thou shalt make thy way prosperous, and then thou shalt have good success."*

2. WRITE YOUR BUSINESS VISION

In order to start and run your business effectively and profitably, you have to write down a plan to follow. If you don't do this, then you won't have a clear direction to follow to a set destination. And this is not good. Therefore, write your business plan, and conduct feasibility studies. When you want to build a house, you will first get an architect to design the plan of the building. Do the same for your business. Have a blueprint.

Proverbs 29:18

> *"Where there is no vision, the people perish: but he that keepeth the law, happy is he."*

Habakkuk 2:2–3

> [2]*And the LORD answered me, and said, 'Write the vision, and make it plain upon tables, that he may run that readeth it.*
>
> [3]*For the vision is yet for an appointed time, but at the end it shall speak, and not lie: though it tarry, wait for it; because it will surely come, it will not tarry.*

3. COUNT THE COST OF THE BUSINESS.

Jesus was a great business person. He said in,

Luke 2:49

> *"And he said unto them, How is it that ye sought me? Wist ye not that I must be about my Father's business?"*

Jesus advised that before you start a project or business, you should cost it to ascertain if you have enough money to finish it. You must do this in order to avoid uncompleted or abandoned projects.

Luke 14:28–30

> [28]*For which of you, intending to build a tower, sitteth not down first, and counteth the cost, whether he have sufficient to finish it?*

> [29]*Lest haply, after he hath laid the foundation, and is not able to finish it, all that behold it begin to mock him,*
>
> [30]*Saying, This man began to build, and was not able to finish.*

Your business plan should contain a cash flow forecast of your income and expenditure. Your estimated costs must be determined. After an architect has designed a building, a quantity surveyor will find out the cost of building. Do the same for your business. Have estimated cost for your project or business.

4. ACCOUNTABILITY

Jesus had a treasurer, Judas for His ministry. Businesses hire accountants. The reason for this is for proper accountability. You must keep proper records for your business so that you can truly know how your business is doing. Ensure that your expenses are always lower than your income so that you can operate at a profit.

5. PROFITABILITY

You are in business to make profit. Therefore, you must keep depending on God to teach you how to make profit. And this means you will continually inquire from the Lord to teach you ways to make profit.

Isaiah 48:17

> *"Thus saith the Lord, thy Redeemer, the Holy One of Israel; I am the Lord thy God which teacheth thee to profit, which leadeth thee by the way that thou shouldest go."*

Proverbs 14:23

> *"In all labour there is profit: but the talk of the lips tendeth only to penury."*

When you ask God in prayers He will show you how to make profit, how to diversify, where to get raw materials, staff to hire, location of your business, and when to expand, etc.

6. HONESTY AND INTEGRITY

As a Christian business person, you must determine to do your business honestly. And this means you have to do a legal business. No illegal stuff. Register your business, and pay your ***tax***. Sell quality products. Charge reasonable prices for your products and services, and don't rip people off.

Psalms 25:21

> *"Let integrity and uprightness preserve me; for I wait on thee."*

Proverbs 22:1

> *"A good name is rather to be chosen than great riches, and loving favour rather than silver and gold."*

Integrity and a good name is an asset. Build it and protect it. It's greater than riches. Let people trust your words, goods, and services.

Proverbs 10:22

> *"The blessing of the Lord, it maketh rich, and he addeth no sorrow with it."*

7. DON'T DEFRAUD ANYONE

As a Christian business person, you must determine not to defraud or deceive anyone in order to make money.

Proverbs 10:22

> *"The blessing of the Lord, it maketh rich, and he addeth no sorrow with it."*

When you make money by defrauding people, it's not a blessing because sorrow will be added to it. The Bible also says in the scripture below that when people make money dubiously, such money dwindles. Therefore, make money in an upright way without defrauding anyone.

Proverbs 13:11

"Wealth gotten by vanity shall be diminished: but he that gathereth by labour shall increase."

8. GIVE YOUR TITHE

As a Christian business person, you have to connect to the prosperity of God through your tithing. Tithe is ten percent of your ***gross*** earnings.

Note that tithe is not a tax, neither is it meant to decrease you financially. Tithe will actually bring forth financial increase for you if you do it correctly. See Malachi 3:10.

Leviticus 27:30-32

30*And all the tithe of the land, whether of the seed of the land, or of the fruit of the tree, is the LORD'S: it is holy unto the Lord.*

31*And if a man will at all redeem ought of his tithes, he shall add thereto the fifth part thereof.*

32*And concerning the tithe of the herd, or of the flock, even of whatsoever passeth under the rod, the tenth shall be holy unto the LORD.*

Proverbs 3:9-10

9*Honour the Lord with thy substance, and with the firstfruits of all thine increase:*

10*So shall thy barns be filled with plenty, and thy presses shall burst out with new wine.*

9. DILIGENCE

Business is not for lazy people. In order to succeed, you must be diligent. You must be prepared to put in a lot of hours into your business for it to be fully established.

Proverbs 10:4

> *"He becometh poor that dealeth with a slack hand: but the hand of the diligent maketh rich."*

Proverbs 22:29

> *"Seest thou a man diligent in his business? he shall stand before kings; he shall not stand before mean men."*

10. HAVE A MENTOR

A mentor is a highly trusted, knowledgeable, skilled, and experienced person who knows a lot about what you want to do, know or learn. A mentor is a coach. Find a coach who you should follow and he will teach you things in your chosen field. With the help of your mentor, you will make less mistakes or even none, and achieve a lot in a short time. Examples of Mentors and Mentees in the Bible are: Moses and Joshua; Saul and David; Naomi and Ruth; Mordecai and Esther; Paul and Timothy; and Jesus and the twelve disciples.

11. PRAYERS

You surely need to pray regularly both in understanding and in tongues for yourself and your business. Your effectual fervent prayers will avail much for you. You also have to study the Bible regularly, as well as praise and worship God continually.

CHAPTER SIXTY-TWO

HARD TRUTH – VOWS AND PLEDGES– ECCLESIASTES 5:4–6

Here is what happened during a ministration in a church. Note that the call to support a church building project financially is entirely voluntary. No pressures!

PASTOR: Who will support the building fund of the church with £2,000 and make sure you give it now or bring it to church within the next three days?

MEMBERS: Meeeeeee!

PASTOR: Please only come forward to the altar for prayer and anointing if you are sure you will give the money now or bring it within the next three days.

MEMBERS: Loads of members starts coming forward including those who don't have the money now, and those who do not intend to bring it within three days even if they have it because they consider the money to be too much. Note that some who don't have the money now will say, "I'm exercising my faith." But faith becomes foolish if you vow or pledge to God something far too much to fulfil.

My friend, for your information, vows and pledges to God is a serious business. It's no joke. Therefore, never vow or pledge anything to God that you are not prepared to fulfil. According to the Bible, it is foolishness to do so. Besides, the person will end up destroying the work of his own hands by so doing. In fact, it is far better not to make a vow or pledge to God or even to a fellow human being, than promising and not fulfiling it.

Some do it because perhaps they want to show off to other members that they have so much money, and they don't. My friend, humble yourself before God and be seated if you don't have the £2,000. It's more honourable and rewarding for you to be seated. Some do it out of emotions. Some do it to trick the Pastor thinking the money will end up in the Pastor's pocket. They will say, "He will not see the money." My friend, the vow or pledge is to God and towards God's building project. Whatever the reason may be, read the following scriptures and draw your own conclusion.

Ecclesiastes 5:4–6

> [4]*When thou vowest a vow unto God, defer not to pay it; for he hath no pleasure in fools: pay that which thou hast vowed.*
>
> [5]*Better is it that thou shouldest not vow, than that thou shouldest vow and not pay.*
>
> [6]*Suffer not thy mouth to cause thy flesh to sin; neither say thou before the angel, that it was an error: wherefore should God be angry at thy voice, and destroy the work of thine hands?*

Today, calculate all the vows and pledges you owe God and redeem them immediately. And never make any more vows and pledges you are not prepared to fulfil. God can destroy the work of a person's hand as a result. Learn from the Psalmist. He says in,

Psalms 66:13-14

> [13]*I will go into thy house with burnt offerings: I will pay thee my vows,*
>
> [14]*Which my lips have uttered, and my mouth hath spoken, when I was in trouble.*

Pledging without fulfiling it will put the person in bondage, and to pay it will bring forth freedom and healing.

CHAPTER SIXTY-THREE

WHAT DEFILES A MAN? –MARK 7:20–23

A number of things can defile a man. However, I will like to mainly dwell on what the Bible says defiles a man. Our Lord Jesus tells us in the scripture below the things that defile a man. To defile means to make unclean, impure, or corrupt. This message is important in order for us to continually do things that will keep us pure and healthy. Basically, according to the scriptures, defilement can happen in three main ways discussed below.

1. Through the things that we dwell on which proceed from our heart.
2. Through bitterness.
3. Through fornication.

Mark 7:20–23

> 20*And he said, That which cometh out of the man, that defileth the man.*
>
> 21*For from within, out of the heart of men, proceed evil thoughts, adulteries, fornications, murders.*
>
> 22*Thefts, covetousness, wickedness, deceit, lasciviousness, an evil eye, blasphemy, pride, foolishness:*
>
> 23*All these evil things come from within, and defile the man.*

The first time I read the above scripture, I was surprised to know that it's not the things that we eat and drink that defile us, but rather the things that proceed from within out of our hearts as mentioned above by our Lord Jesus Christ. It's therefore important for us to refrain from dwelling on the above things that defile a man so that there won't be need for healing. Prevention is better than cure.

Instead of dwelling on the things that defile, the solution is to do what ***Philippians 4:8*** says,

> *"Finally, brethren, whatsoever things are true, whatsoever things are honest, whatsoever things are just, whatsoever things are pure, whatsoever things are lovely, whatsoever things are of good report; if there be any virtue, and if there be any praise, think on these things."*

Hebrews 12:15

> *"Looking diligently lest any man fail of the grace of God; lest any root of bitterness springing up trouble you, and thereby many be defiled;"*

According to the above scripture, bitterness is another thing that defiles a man. Before a man gets bitter, it's likely that anger, disappointments, bereavement or some other forms of emotional pain may have happened. The purpose of this message is to guard against defilement which will make a man to need healing.

1 Corinthians 6:18–19

> 18 *Flee fornication. Every sin that a man doeth is without the body; but he that committeth fornication sinneth against his own body.*
>
> 19 *What? know ye not that your body is the temple of the Holy Ghost which is in you, which ye have of God, and ye are not your own?*

1 Corinthians 3:16–17

> 16 *Know ye not that ye are the temple of God, and that the Spirit of God dwelleth in you?*
>
> 17 *If any man defile the temple of God, him shall God destroy; for the temple of God is holy, which temple ye are.*

Many years ago in Nigeria in the mid 80's, there was this rich man, Emeka who was a car spare parts dealer. He was also a womaniser having many girlfriends. As a result of his many relationships with women, his body was corrupted and he started increasing in size mysteriously to the extent that he suddenly blew up to twice his normal size. The oracle and the gods were consulted as well as a Man of God, and he was said to have committed adultery with a married woman that's why he was afflicted with that incurable disease. Meanwhile, he spent all his money on hospital treatment and did not get any better. His business was completely ruined. It was not long and he died. This is just an example of what sexual immorality can do to a man.

From the above scriptures you can see that the sin of fornication is sin against that person's own body, and that is defilement of the temple of God, and the Bible says God will destroy that person because the temple of God is Holy, and that person is the temple. The sin of fornication is like shooting yourself. Deadly! Sodom and Gomorrah city was wiped out by God because of sexual immorality.

CHAPTER SIXTY-FOUR

LEVELS OF FAITH

The Bible gives us the meaning of faith in ***Hebrews 11:1*** saying, "*Now faith is the substance of things hoped for, the evidence of things not seen.*"

From ***Romans 12:3*** we also know that, "*...God hath dealt to every man the measure of faith.*" As long you don't use this measure of faith God has given to you, it will remain dormant. The extent to which you use the measure of faith you have also determines your level of faith which is discussed below. The Bible says that faith without works is dead. Therefore, it's important for us to use our faith to the maximum. God is pleased when we use our faith. That's why the Bible says in ***Hebrews 11:6*** that, "*But without faith it is impossible to please him: for he that cometh to God must believe that he is, and that he is a rewarder of them that diligently seek him.*"

SO GREAT FAITH

Jesus described the Centurion as a person with so great faith. His servant was sick and he came to Jesus for help. And Jesus told him that He will come to his house, but he said to Jesus that he is not worthy that He should come under his roof, and that He should just speak the word and he will believe. ***Matthew 8:10*** says, "*When Jesus heard it, he marvelled, and said to them that followed, Verily I say unto you, I have not found so great faith, no, not in Israel.*"

GREAT FAITH

Jesus also described the Woman of Canaan as a person with great faith. Her daughter was seriously sick and she came to Jesus for help. And Jesus said it is not good that the bread meant for the children should be given to dogs. And she answered and said, "*Truth, Lord: yet the dogs eat of the crumbs which fall from their master's table.*" Jesus answered her in ***Matthew 15:28*** saying, "*Then Jesus answered and said unto her, O woman, great is thy faith: be it unto thee even as thou wilt. And her daughter was made whole from that very hour.*"

LITTLE FAITH

Peter and the other disciples saw Jesus walking on water and they marvelled. And Peter requested if he should come, and Jesus said he should come. Initially, Peter walked on water, as long as he focused on Jesus, but when he saw the boisterous wind, he cried out for help and started sinking. Read what Jesus said to him below:

Matthew 14:31

> "*And immediately Jesus stretched forth his hand, and caught him, and said unto him, O thou of little faith, wherefore didst thou doubt?*"

NO FAITH

There are people who don't use the measure of faith God has given them at all in certain circumstances. The scripture below gives us the response Jesus gave to his disciples when they were facing a raging storm and they were fearful and cried out for His help. As long as you don't use your faith, it will remain dormant. When a man regularly works out in the gym, his muscles will be built up. Similarly, the more you use your faith, the more your faith will be built up. Use your faith regularly, and it will be built up to the highest level of – So great faith!

Mark 4:40

> "*And he said unto them, Why are ye so fearful? how is it that ye have no faith?*"

YOUR FAITH HAS MADE YOU WHOLE

Reading the story in the two passages below concerning the Woman with the issue of blood, and Blind Bartimaeus, you will see what Jesus said, "*Thy faith hath made thee whole.*" This means that their healing and wholesomeness largely depended on them using their faith without which nothing would have happened. They put their faith into action. Similarly, if you don't start using your faith regarding what you want from God, it's likely nothing will happen because as we saw earlier in ***Hebrews 11:6***, "*But without faith it is impossible to please him:*"

Mark 5:34,

> [34]"*And he said unto her, Daughter, thy faith hath made thee whole; go in peace, and be whole of thy plague.*"

Mark 10:52

> [52]"And Jesus said *unto him, Go thy way; thy faith hath made thee whole. And immediately he received his sight, and followed Jesus in the way.*"

It's important for us to know the different levels of faith so that we can start using our faith properly. Use so great faith in situations like the Centurion and see miracles happen. It's also interesting to note that we don't need big faith to get things done. As a matter of fact, Jesus said all we need is faith as small as a mustard seed in order to move mountains in ***Matthew 17:20,***

> "*And Jesus said unto them, Because of your unbelief: for verily I say unto you, If ye have faith as a grain of mustard seed, ye shall say unto this mountain, Remove hence to yonder place; and it shall remove; and nothing shall be impossible unto you.*"

Also, if we claim to have faith, and we don't have evidence to prove it, such faith is dead. ***James 2:17*** says, "*Even so faith, if it hath not works, is dead, being alone.*"

CHAPTER SIXTY-FIVE

THE POWER OF GOD

The power of God is awesome. The power of God is supernatural. The power of God is extraordinary. The power of God is marvellous. The power of God is instant. The power of God is miraculous. Some people depend on all sorts of fake power to help them. For example, some depend on their gods, charms, cult, gang, fat bank account balance, Godfather, etc. The power of God helps to heal and restore health. Therefore, we must learn to depend on God.

THE POWER OF GOD HEALS.

In Mark 5:26-34, the tremendous power of God was made available to heal the woman who had an issue of blood for twelve years instantly.

In Mark 1:29-31, Peter's mother-in-law was healed of fever instantly through the tremendous power of God.

In Mark 2:1-12, the man sick of the palsy carried by his four friends to Jesus experienced immediate power of God which put him up again on his feet.

In Luke 13:10-13, the power of God was made available to heal instantly the woman with the spirit of infirmity for eighteen years.

In John 5:1-9, the man with an infirmity for thirty-eight years by the pool was instantly healed.

As the anointed servant of the Most High God, I declare that heaven will open up to you now to heal you of any pain, sickness, or disease in the name of Jesus Christ of Nazareth!

THE POWER OF GOD DELIVERS FROM BONDAGE.

In Daniel 3:19-30, the tremendous power of God preserved the three Hebrew boys Shadrach, Meshach, and Abednego (SMA) from death in the fire of the fiery furnace.

In Acts 16:23-26 the supernatural power of God manifested in prison through a great earthquake to set Paul and Silas free.

Today, I declare with every authority in the name of Jesus Christ of Nazareth, let chains, fetters, and bondage fall off and be destroyed by Holy Ghost fire. You are free indeed.

THE POWER OF GOD MAKES A WAY

The power of God makes a way even where there seems to be no way. In Exodus 14:13-21, the extraordinary power of God through a strong east wind divided the red sea for the Israelites to be delivered from their enemies – the Egyptians. I declare through the awesome power of God, and in the name of my Lord Jesus that you shall indeed experience immediate open doors. The siege is over now. The walls of Jericho are surely coming down now in Jesus' name. Amen!

THE POWER OF GOD QUICKENS THE DEAD.

In John chapter 11, Lazarus was pronounced dead, buried, and was in the tomb for four days. And then the power of God manifested through our Lord Jesus. And he that was dead was quickened and restored back to life. Are there things you consider dead and lifeless? Today, the tremendous power of God is available in full measure to restore everything in Jesus' name. Amen!

THE POWER OF GOD MANIFESTS EVERYWHERE.

Finally, the power of God manifests everywhere. Therefore, there is absolutely no barrier to the manifestation of the power of God. For example, in Matthew 8:5-13, the Centurion had an understanding and revelation about the power of God. When Jesus told him, I will come and heal your servant, read below what he said.

Matthew 8:8

> *"The centurion answered and said, Lord, I am not worthy that thou shouldest come under my roof: but speak the word only, and my servant shall be healed."*

Today, the power of God will touch and infuse you right now in your home to heal, deliver, restore, strengthen, open new doors of divine opportunities and establish you forever. The power of God will touch and infuse you now in your office, in the car, train, ship, shop, and anywhere you may be to cause you to be free indeed. The power of God working for you will produce testimonies for you in Jesus' name. Amen!

CHAPTER SIXTY-SIX

MEDICAL PERIODIC CHECK UPS

Healing can sometimes be by a combination of the spiritual and medical science. They work hand in hand to achieve the same result – healing. This means that we have to pay attention to our health and go for periodic check-ups in advance in order to highlight any health concerns. Prevention is better than cure. It is by far easier to treat, control, and effectively cure sicknesses and diseases at an early stage than when it is full blown. Therefore, do blood tests, urine test, dental care, eye test, kidney test, cholesterol test, blood pressure test, breast cancer check-up, prostate cancer check-up etc. These tests will reveal any concerns on time, and treatment administered to cure it.

Apart from doing periodic medical check-ups, it is also advisable to adhere to your doctor's advice, and follow his instructions. The same thing applies in the area of medication. Take your medication according to prescription. And report any side effects, allergies, or reactions immediately. Some people indulge in what I call, 'foolish faith.' They discontinue the use of their medication and the sickness gets worse. It's perfectly fine if for example, somebody has a revelation or a leading of the Holy Spirit to discontinue their medication and they go ahead to do so by faith.

Medical science has existed right from Bible days. For example, Luke, the author of the gospel according to Luke, was a Physician. Balm and Physicians have been in existence from the Old Testament days.

Jeremiah 8:21-22

> 21*For the hurt of the daughter of my people am I hurt; I am black; astonishment hath taken hold on me.*

> [22]*Is there no balm in Gilead; is there no physician there? why then is not the health of the daughter of my people recovered?*

Even when you receive some spiritual healing, it is still advisable to have a medical check-up for further confirmation. For example, If a person has been healed through holy communion, or anointing oil, it is advisable to still see the Doctor. Let the Doctors check you out with their medical equipment and confirm you to be fine.

CHAPTER SIXTY-SEVEN

BODILY EXERCISE PROFITS LITTLE – 1 TIMOTHY 4:8

As good as going to the gym to work out is, or doing various kinds of sport to keep fit is, the Bible says it profits little. No book is as authentic as the Holy Bible. If it says it, then it is true.

1 Timothy 4:8 says,

> *"For bodily exercise profiteth little: but godliness is profitable unto all things, having promise of the life that now is, and of that which is to come."*

According to the above scripture, godliness is profitable unto all things. Godliness is spiritual exercise and it involves the following:

1. Studying the Bible.
2. Meditating on the Word of God.
3. Obeying the Word of God – Bible.
5. Praying and praising God.
6. Abstaining from sin.
7. Be a worker in the vineyard of the Lord and participate fully in church activities.
8. Be a soul winner– Evangelise.
9. Be a person of faith, always acting on the Word of God.
10. Always walking in love.

Psalm 37:4

> 4 *"Delight thyself also in the* L*ORD: and he shall give thee the desires of thine heart."*

These days some people are real exercise freaks, having good physique and muscles, but their spirit and soul are never looked after. Man is essentially a spirit being. Therefore, we have to pay more attention looking after our spirit. Unfortunately, the reverse is the case. The body is more looked after than the spirit and soul. Today, get into the spiritual gym and start working out spiritually using the above listed ten tools and you will be sharpened spiritually. You need a balanced outlook, spirit, soul, and body.

CHAPTER SIXTY-EIGHT

GIVE YOURSELF A TREAT – CELEBRATE!

One of the best things you can do for yourself is to have a good break and give yourself a treat. Relax and celebrate! Lively up yourself! Go on a shopping spree for yourself. Go on holiday abroad with your partner and stay in a posh hotel. Have a cruise in a ship. Have a lot of romance, love and sex to refresh your soul. Play your favourite music. Watch your favourite movie. See a nice theatre performance. Put on your best clothes and jewellery. Eat your favourite food, and drink your favourite non-alcoholic wine and have a merry heart. Play with your family and friends.

Take your dog out for a walk in a beautiful park and breathe some fresh air there. Go for sightseeing to nice important places. Go to the museum or art gallery and see beautiful art works and costumes. Go to the zoo and see animals and appreciate the animal kingdom. Go to a party, sing and dance. Go to gym and exercise. Watch your favourite sports game on television. Visualise a beautiful life for yourself. Have a laugh. Draw and do some painting. Pamper yourself. Life is too short. All these will enhance your healing and help you remain healthy.

Part of giving yourself a treat is also to have proper rest for the body after periods of hard work. Take a break and go on holiday. Have a sabbatical. Even Jesus had time to rest and sleep in a ship as recorded in ***Mark 4:38***, *"And he was in the hinder part of the ship, asleep on a pillow: and they awake him, and say unto him, Master, carest thou not that we perish?"*

Jesus recognised that rest is important for the body. He asked His disciples to go and rest in ***Mark 6:31*** *saying, "And he said unto them, Come ye yourselves apart into a desert place, and rest* *a while: for there were many coming and going, and they had no leisure so much as to eat."*

When the body is overworked it appears sickly, needing rest to recuperate. Proper rest that you give to your body will help bring forth healing and restore health and vitality. To balance this message, I will like to also mention here that the body also needs work. Laziness will corrupt the body and make it sickly. Therefore, also take pleasure in working, but not too much that will make the body breakdown.

You are not being selfish because you gave yourself a treat. After all, you have been doing things for people. Do for yourself too. You are the one working hard to earn the money. Love your neighbour as you love yourself. That love begins with you. Charity begins at home. Not outside. To spoil yourself will give you memorable times to dwell on when you have a reflection about life and it will make you smile, and laugh.

Ecclesiastes 5:18–19

> [18]*Behold that which I have seen: it is good and comely for one to eat and to drink, and to enjoy the good of all his labour that he taketh under the sun all the days of his life, which God giveth him: for it is his portion.*
>
> [19]*Every man also to whom God hath given riches and wealth, and hath given him power to eat thereof, and to take his portion, and to rejoice in his labour; this is the gift of God.*

Joel 2:26

> [26]*"And ye shall eat in plenty, and be satisfied, and praise the name of the LORD your God, that hath dealt wondrously with you: and my people shall never be ashamed."*

Give yourself a treat. Enjoy! Celebrate! Jesus came to give you life, and give it to you more abundantly. Enjoy that abundant life without restrictions. Study and meditate on the Word of God. Praise and worship God. ***Philippians 4:4*** *says, "Rejoice in the Lord alway: and again I say, Rejoice."*

CHAPTER SIXTY-NINE

GOD IS A MASTER PLANNER–JEREMIAH 29:11

Before the foundations of the world, God determined your creation and existence, as well as what your purpose will be on earth. He said in ***Jeremiah* 1:5**, *"Before I formed thee in the belly I knew thee; and before thou camest forth out of the womb I sanctified thee, and I ordained thee a prophet unto the nations."*

Before God formed Prophet Jeremiah in his mother's womb, He sanctified and ordained him to be a Prophet to nations. The same thing applies to us. Our purpose on earth has already been defined. All we are meant to do is discover our purpose and walk in the path and will of God for us. If for example, God has ordained that somebody should be a Pastor, and they go ahead to become a Medical Doctor it will be hard for them to have a fulfilled life. And God Himself may also stir them up and redirect their plans to be in line with His will for them.

God sent Prophet Jonah to go and preach in Nineveh, but he refused and wanted to escape to Tarshish, and God cornered him and sent a fish to swallow him up for three days. While in the fish belly, he prayed for God's mercy and repented. That's a trial to get him to accomplish God's purpose for him. When he was vomited by the fish, he immediately ran to Nineveh and preached. This shows that God can even allow us to go through some trials in order for us to fall in line with His original plan for us. ***Jeremiah* 29:11 NIV**, *"For I know the plans I have for you, declares the* Lord, *plans to prosper you and not to harm you, plans to give you hope and a future."*

As long as we don't discover our purpose on earth and follow it, living life will seem hellish, when in fact we are meant to enjoy life. ***Proverbs 19:21 NIV,*** *"Many are the plans in a person's heart, but it is the LORD's purpose that prevails."*

There are many times that we make our own plans, but such plans are sure to fail if we don't consult God first, and if it is not His will for us. We should be thankful to God rather than lament when such selfish unapproved plans fail. God always has better plans for us. Follow the blueprint God has made for your life and have a joy filled fulfilled life.

CHAPTER SEVENTY

GO IN THE WAY OF PEACE

To always go in the way of peace is great because it will bring forth progress and prosperity. When there is a dispute, for peace to reign, it requires the efforts of the two people or parties involved. Peace is not cheap. There is a price to pay if you have to seek and pursue peace as the Bible states. Part of the price to pay is that you will have to throw away your pride and humble yourself to be reconciled to the other party. It means that you may have to say, "Sorry" even if you are right. It means that you may have to compromise on your values. It also means you have to ignore and forgive a lot of things.

The Bible says in ***Psalms 34:14***, *"Depart from evil, and do good; seek peace, and pursue it."* To seek peace and pursue it shows that peace is not cheap. In the process of seeking and pursuing peace, if you were cheated, you may have to allow yourself to be cheated and forgive. There is a price to pay. But the truth is that when you eventually establish peace, after paying a high price, it is certainly worth it.

Living in harmony is good, but you certainly cannot force peace. Peace should indeed be mutual. What will you do if you try to make peace and it is not working? The truth remains that there are some relationships that have broken down so terribly, because trust is gone. Commit such relationships to God and maybe His mercy or perhaps time will heal such relationships. Take solace in the scripture below in the meantime while you seek and pursue peace in seemingly irreconcilable relationship. ***Romans 12:18*** says, *"If it be possible, as much as lieth in you, live peaceably with all men."* Note the word "If." The Bible says, *"If it be possible,..."* indicating that it may be impossible to reconcile and be at peace with some people. For example, there are relationships people find themselves in which one party is always right and the other party is always wrong. Again, some people may be wrong but they may never admit it, neither will they say, "Sorry." And some people are simply unrepentant in the sense that they keep breaching the peace process.

Philippians 4:6–7,

> [6]*Be careful for nothing; but in everything by prayer and supplication with thanksgiving let your requests be made known unto God.*
>
> [7]*And the peace of God, which passeth all understanding, shall keep your hearts and minds through Christ Jesus.*

We all need the peace that surpasses all understanding. That is the peace that truly brings forth healing. Keep up with your prayers, supplications, and thanksgiving to God.

To go in the way of peace also means that you have to continually check your spirit and follow the leading of the Holy Spirit as you make decisions. Follow your intuitions. If you don't have peace regarding a plan or an issue, it's an indication that it doesn't have the approval of God and you should therefore pull out immediately. But if you feel the perfect peace of God that surpasses all understanding, it's a green light that you may go ahead. Let God always guide and direct you in all you do.

Psalm 32:8

> [8]*"I will instruct thee and teach thee in the way which thou shalt go: I will guide thee with mine eye."*

Hebrews 12:14,

> *"Follow peace with all men, and holiness, without which no man shall see the Lord:"*

No matter what happens, always try to go in the way of peace knowing that without peace and holiness no man shall see the Lord or be in heaven.

CHAPTER SEVENTY-ONE

THE WAGES OF SIN – ROMANS 6:23

This is not to scare anyone but the truth is that the wages of sin is death, and this truth is documented in the scripture below. Knowing that sin has deadly consequence should act as a deterrent to any wise Christian to refrain from meddling with sin or making sin a lifestyle. To live a sin free life will bring forth healing and good health. ***Romans 6:23***, *"For the wages of sin is death; but the gift of God is eternal life through Jesus Christ our Lord."*

God is angry with the wicked every day. This scripture is a warning to the wicked to repent from their evil ways so that God's daily anger will not be aggravated. ***Psalm 7:11***, *"God judgeth the righteous, and God is angry with the wicked every day."*

King Solomon, the wise king of Israel tells us in the scripture below that the reason why the hearts of men are fully set to do evil is because the penalty against evil work is not executed speedily. Men are unrepentant from their sinful ways because they know God is merciful.

Ecclesiastics 8:11

> *"Because sentence against an evil work is not executed speedily, therefore the heart of the sons of men is fully set in them to do evil."*

The scripture below further clarifies the deadly effects of sin. In just three verses below, Prophet Isaiah hit the nail on the head of the consequences of sin to man. It's now down to us to try to avoid sin as much as possible.

Isaiah 59:1–3

> *[1]Behold, the LORD's hand is not shortened, that it cannot save; neither his ear heavy, that it cannot hear:*
>
> *[2]But your iniquities have separated between you and your God, and your sins have hid his face from you, that he will not hear.*
>
> *[3]For your hands are defiled with blood, and your fingers with iniquity; your lips have spoken lies, your tongue hath muttered perverseness.*

Hebrews 11:24-25

> *[24]By faith Moses, when he was come to years, refused to be called the son of Pharaoh's daughter;*
>
> *[25]Choosing rather to suffer affliction with the people of God, than to enjoy the pleasures of sin for a season;*

The Bible says in the above scripture that Moses refused to enjoy the pleasures of sin. In Luke 16:19–31, the rich man enjoyed the pleasures of sin by not helping Lazarus as he ought to while on earth, and he died and ended up in hell.

CHAPTER SEVENTY-TWO

AND GOD REMEMBERED ME

As you read this message, I prophesy to you that the Lord will remember you for good and grant you all your heart desires in line with His will for you in Jesus' name. Sometimes, we live life and pass through the wilderness and some trials during which time it seems the Lord had forgotten the person. Not anymore because your time has come to be remembered and favoured in Jesus' name. Zion actually said in the scripture below that the Lord has forsaken and forgotten him. And the next verse says that even if a woman forgets to breastfeed her son, the Lord will never forget to help His children. And another scripture says He will never leave us nor forsake us.

Isaiah 49:14–15

> [14]*But Zion said, The LORD hath forsaken me, and my Lord hath forgotten me.*
>
> [15]*Can a woman forget her sucking child, that she should not have compassion on the son of her womb? yea, they may forget, yet will I not forget thee.*

When God remembers somebody, it is usually for good. Such goodies may even come in quick succession amounting to overflow and causing you to give Him glory by testifying. Let's look at a few scriptures below to see what happened to people God remembered. Another interesting thing about God remembering a person is that God can also divinely quicken a person to remember you. The Bible says that God remembered Noah and everything in the ark, and caused wind to blow on the earth and the waters subsided. ***Genesis 8:1*** says, "*And God remembered Noah, and* *every living thing, and all the cattle that was with him in the ark: and God made a wind to pass over the earth, and the waters assuaged;"*

When God remembered Rachel, her womb was opened and she gave birth to Joseph in Genesis 30:22 that says, "*And God remembered Rachel, and God hearkened to her, and opened her womb.*"

God remembered Hannah, and barrenness was ended as she conceived and gave birth to Samuel in ***1 Samuel 1:19–20*** that says,

> [19]*And they rose up in the morning early, and worshipped before the LORD, and returned, and came to their house to Ramah: and Elkanah knew Hannah his wife; and the LORD remembered her.*
>
> [20]*Wherefore it came to pass, when the time was come about after Hannah had conceived, that she bare a son, and called his name Samuel, saying, Because I have asked him of the LORD.*

God will make your destiny helpers to have sleepless nights and help you as He made King Ahasuerus, and stirred him up to help Mordecai. ***Esther 6:1-3*** says,

> [1] *On that night could not the king sleep, and he commanded to bring the book of records of the chronicles; and they were read before the king.*
>
> [2]*And it was found written, that Mordecai had told of Bigthana and Teresh, two of the king's chamberlains, the keepers of the door, who sought to lay hand on the king Ahasuerus.*
>
> [3]*And the king said, What honour and dignity hath been done to Mordecai for this? Then said the king's servants that ministered unto him, There is nothing done for him.*

Read Esther 6:4-14 for the rest of the story and see how Mordecai was arrayed with royal apparel and paraded on the streets in a majestic style.

God can also remember you by quickening a wicked person to help you. God used Evil Merodach King of Babylon to release

King Johoiachin of Judah out of prison after thirty-seven years in ***2 kings 25:27-30,***

> [27]*And it came to pass in the seven and thirtieth year of the captivity of Jehoiachin king of Judah, in the twelfth month, on the seven and twentieth day of the month, that Evil Merodach king of Babylon in the year that he began to reign did lift up the head of Jehoiachin king of Judah out of prison;*
>
> [28]*And he spake kindly to him, and set his throne above the throne of the kings that were with him in Babylon;*
>
> [29]*And changed his prison garments: and he did eat bread continually before him all the days of his life.*
>
> [30]*And his allowance was a continual allowance given him of the king, a daily rate for every day, all the days of his life.*

Note that you can also pray for God to remember you if it appears to be that you have been forgotten. Let's look at people who prayed for God to remember them.

The Philistines captured Samson, bound him with fetters of brass, and put out his two eyes. Painful! He cried out to God in prayers in ***Judges 16:28*** saying, "*And Samson called unto the LORD, and said, O Lord God, remember me, I pray thee, and strengthen me, I pray thee, only this once, O God, that I may be at once avenged of the Philistines for my two eyes.*"

After Nehemiah had worked hard doing good deeds in the house of the Lord he prayed in ***Nehemiah 13:14*** saying, "*Remember me, O my God, concerning this, and wipe not out my good deeds that I have done for the house of my God, and for the offices thereof*". See also Nehemiah 13:22, 29, and 31.

Perhaps you have sowed offerings, tithes, and donations in the house of the Lord and you have also helped people through charity but you are not seeing the rewards. You can also pray to God to remember you for a bountiful harvest. King David prayed in ***Psalm 20:3*** saying, "*Remember all thy offerings, and accept thy burnt sacrifice; Selah.*"

Finally, I will like to mention here that all we truly have to do for God to remember us is just for us to have a pure heart. Hold no grudge, avoid bitterness, envy, and jealousy and have a loving pure heart and you will definitely be the next on line for God to remember and visit you with goodies in Jesus' name. Amen!

CHAPTER SEVENTY-THREE

GOD IS NOT A MAN THAT HE SHOULD LIE – NUMBERS 23:19

Our God is a faithful God. Whatever He has promised you, He will certainly fulfil. Though it may tarry, wait for it patiently to manifest at the appointed time. The Bible says in ***Numbers 23:19***, "*God is not a man, that he should lie; neither the son of man, that he should repent: hath he said, and shall he not do it? or hath he spoken, and shall he not make it good?*"

Even if it is the precious promises in the Word of God you are holding on to, He will bring it to pass in your life provided you don't doubt. ***Romans 3:4*** says, "*God forbid: yea, let God be true, but every man a liar; as it is written, That thou mightest be justified in thy sayings, and mightest overcome when thou art judged.*"

Has God given you a prophetic word, or revealed something to you in a vision, or dream? Wait patiently for it to manifest. If you have been waiting so eagerly, it is likely to manifest when you probably give up on waiting for it, and forgotten about it. That's God for you. Sarah was already 89 years old when God spoke saying she will give birth to a son after she has long gone past her menopause. The Bible recorded that Sarah laughed because it sounded ridiculous to her and impossible. Well, Sarah went ahead and had Isaac as God said. That's to show that with God all things are possible.

Genesis 18:11-12

> 11*Now Abraham and Sarah were old and well stricken in age; and it ceased to be with Sarah after the manner of women.*
>
> 12*Therefore Sarah laughed within herself, saying, After I am waxed old shall I have pleasure, my lord being old also?*

God does not use perfect people to accomplish His mission. The more unfit and unlikely you appear to be, the better because He is out to do something great through you to showcase His power and glory through you. When God called Gideon to save Israel from the Midianites, he made excuses and cried out saying in ***Judges 6:15-16,***

> 15*And he said unto him, Oh my Lord, wherewith shall I save Israel? behold, my family is poor in Manasseh, and I am the least in my father's house.*
>
> 16*And the LORD said unto him, Surely I will be with thee, and thou shalt smite the Midianites as one man.*

Gideon went ahead and successfully led Israel to defeat the Midianites with just 300 men instead of the 32,000 men that turned up initially.

When God called Moses to lead the Israelites out of the land of Egypt, he couldn't believe it. He made excuses saying that he was not eloquent and ***Exodus 4:10-12*** says,

> 10*And Moses said unto the LORD, O my LORD, I am not eloquent, neither heretofore, nor since thou hast spoken unto thy servant: but I am slow of speech, and of a slow tongue.*
>
> 11*And the LORD said unto him, Who hath made man's mouth? or who maketh the dumb, or deaf, or the seeing, or the blind? have not I the LORD?*
>
> 12*Now therefore go, and I will be with thy mouth, and teach thee what thou shalt say.*

Moses went ahead and successfully led the Israelites out of Egypt. God is a master planner. He is a specialist in using the foolish, weak, and despised things of this world to confound the wise and mighty. ***1 Corinthians 1:27–28*** says,

> 27*But God hath chosen the foolish things of the world to confound the wise; and God hath chosen the weak things of the world to confound the things which are mighty;*

> [28]*And base things of the world, and things which are despised, hath God chosen, yea, and things which are not, to bring to nought things that are:*

Titus 1:2 says, "*In hope of eternal life, which* *<u>God, that cannot lie,</u>* *promised before the world began;*"

Finally, any time it appears that what God promised you has not come to pass, don't be quick to attack God, but go and check yourself and find out what you are doing wrong that you need to correct, and then you will see the manifestation of what you desire, because God cannot lie. He is forever faithful to His word. God is not man that He should lie.

CHAPTER SEVENTY-FOUR

GREED KILLS – PROVERBS 1:18–19

Once upon a time, three friends in one African country decided to go to the farm in the jungle to harvest crops. When they got there, they miraculously found a briefcase fully loaded with American dollars. They screamed out in excitement declaring, "What a loss for the white man that owns this briefcase!" They immediately got together and started to make plans on how to share out the spoils.

Meanwhile, they got out a few dollars and asked one of them to go back to town and buy some food to sustain them while in the bush. As this man got out, Satan entered into him, and he started making plans on what he will do to eliminate the other two men, and take all the money alone. He decided he would poison the portion of food meant for the other two men. While he was busy making his plans, the other two men were also busy making their own plan on what they will do to eliminate the man who went to buy food so that two of them will share the money. They decided they will break his head with a strong piece of wood when he returned.

The man returned with the poisoned food for the other two men. They immediately struck him on the head with a strong piece of wood and he fell down and died. They now settled down and ate the poisoned food and after eating they both dropped dead. Greed kills!

The police swung into action to investigate the sudden disappearance of the three men, and they traced them to the farm in the jungle. All three men lay dead and the briefcase full of dollars was beside the men. Greed kills!

What's the lesson to learn from this story? Avoid greed! Any person who always wants to get everything in a business deal or whatever relationship is greedy and he will surely pay with his life one day. Greed kills! Avoid greed like plague. The Bible says in ***Proverbs 1:18-19***,

> [18]*And they lay in wait for their own blood; they lurk privily for their own lives.*
>
> [19]*So are the ways of every one that is greedy of gain; which taketh away the life of the owners thereof.*

CHAPTER SEVENTY-FIVE

FORGIVENESS

Some years ago in England, there was this woman, Kimberley who loved her Volkswagen car so much that she would spend so much time and money servicing and maintaining the car. One winter day when the roads where slippery because of ice, she was on the road and the driver coming behind her skidded and mistakenly hit her car, and her bumper and a small part of the car body was slightly damaged. Kimberley got out of her car and saw the damage and was very angry with the driver who was now pleading with her to forgive him, but she would not listen. She immediately called the Police on her mobile, and got the man's insurance details to make a claim.

The very next day, Kimberley was descending on a hilly London road, and she applied her brake, and it failed her. She went ahead and hit the car in front of her and that one hit another and another. Four cars were involved. They all came out of their cars fuming almost ready to tear her apart for putting their lives in danger through her reckless driving. None of them will listen to her excuse that her brake failed. Thankfully, there were no injuries, but the cars were badly damaged including her adored Volkswagen. They immediately called the Police, and she was tested on the spot to ascertain whether she has gone over the alcohol limit and she passed. All the four drivers got her insurance details to make a claim. She was arrested by the Police for reckless driving.

Forgiveness is a seed, sow it. Sowing and reaping is not limited only to the offerings, donations, and tithes you give in church. It goes beyond that and includes your acts of love, kindness, and forgiveness. Be merciful to people and you will also receive mercy. The Bible says in ***Psalm 18:25***, "*With the merciful thou wilt shew* *thyself merciful; with an upright man thou wilt shew thyself upright;"*

God is so serious about the issue of forgiveness that the Bible had to record in ***Matthew 6:15***, *"But if ye forgive not men their trespasses, neither will your Father forgive your trespasses."* We need to pass the forgiveness test to truly be godly. Besides, forgiveness will help bring forth healing of the soul.

One Saturday evening many years ago in England, Jane was in a groovy mood and she dressed up wearing her best clothes and jewellery ready for a boogie in a nightclub. As she came out walking on the street still within her neighbourhood, a man wearing a balaclava approached her and mugged her, taking her precious jewellery and because she initially resisted, she was stabbed twice and she slumped to the ground and left in a pool of her own blood. An eye witness to the incident immediately called the Police and ambulance and they arrived on the scene within minutes and she was taken straight to the hospital, and then to the theatre for surgery. She survived this attack after being in a coma for several days. However, this attack got her into a state of anger, bitterness, and unforgiveness. It was such a traumatic experience for this young lady. The Police carried out an extensive investigation and in the end they caught the attacker and he was tried in court and sentenced to prison. But Jane remained in emotional pain even after years especially when she sees the scars of the stab wounds. This singular act changed the whole life of this bubbly vibrant young lady. The thought and scars of this fatal incident always reopen the emotional pain suggesting she has not forgiven the attacker.

HOW TO KNOW IF YOU HAVE FORGIVEN THOSE WHO HURT YOU.

1. When you are no longer angry and bitter against them. No more grudges.
2. When you no longer murmur or complain to anybody about what they did wrong.

3. When you no longer have the intention to revenge for what they did wrong.
4. When you no longer wish some terrible evil will befall those who hurt you.
5. When you can experience the perfect peace of God when you remember what they did wrong or when you see them physically.
6. When you no longer bear malice against them, and you can communicate with them freely, fully reconciled to them as if nothing happened in the past. Tread with caution and apply ***wisdom*** and follow the leading of the ***Holy Spirit*** as you become friends with them again.
7. When you can still love them and pray for them as Jesus commanded in ***Matthew 5:44*** saying, *"But I say unto you, love your enemies, bless them that curse you, do good to them that hate you, and pray for them that despitefully use you, and persecute you:"* This scripture is the true test for forgiveness.

Completely ***forget*** what they have done wrong in line with the popular phrase, "Forgive and forget." If you must remember anything, it has to be only positive things about those who hurt you. Forget about the negatives completely. ***Forgive them even when they do not say sorry.***

The benefit and beauty of forgiveness is that the peace, and the power of God will be released unto you abundantly, and the heavens will be opened unto you for unlimited overflowing blessings. Forgive!

CHAPTER SEVENTY-SIX

ALL THINGS WORK TOGETHER FOR GOOD – ROMANS 8:28

Many times in life when we are experiencing severe trials we conclude that the trials are very bad for us, but the truth is that the trials only ***seems*** to be bad, because the Most High God is certainly working out something good for you out of that seemingly bad situation. Just relax and trust God to see you through victoriously.

Kofi Akotua shared a powerful testimony with me some years ago about his immigration status in England. He had been residing in the country illegally for fourteen years after his visa expired. One day while he was on his way to work, a team of Police and Immigration officials caught up with him. They demanded his details and upon confirmation with the Home Office on the spot, it was discovered he has been residing in the country illegally. They immediately commenced plans to forcefully remove him from the country. Kofi was visibly shaken as they took him to the detention camp to start preparing his deportation papers. He lamented and preferred to die rather than go back to Accra with nothing. Meanwhile, he did not want to disclose to the officers that he has a wife and two young children with him in England because they are also residing in the country illegally. While he was in the detention camp, he had suicidal thoughts over and over again. For him, this is the end of the world. Unknown to him, God is working out something good behind the scenes in His favour for him and his family to have their immigration status regularised, and given their indefinite stay.

Sometimes before you gain victory in a situation, you will experience a tremendous shaking, similar to a storm or a monstrous hurricane. The storm may even shake the very foundations of your entire being, but you will not die, and it will rather strengthen you. And for sure, as you go through the storms of life, God is always there with you. ***Isaiah 43:2*** says,

> *"When thou passest through the waters, I will be with thee; and through the rivers, they shall not overflow thee: when thou walkest through the fire, thou shalt not be burned; neither shall the flame kindle upon thee."*

Kofi was eventually taken to Heathrow airport from where he will board a flight to Accra. This was still unknown to his wife. Upon checking his travel documents before departure, one of the officers discovered that the date of birth and photograph did not match with his name. Confusion ensued among the officers, and Kofi was ordered to step aside for the document to be properly verified and cleared and in the process, the flight he was meant to board to Accra took off. One of the officers now told him he could get a Solicitor to stand for him regarding the matter, which he did straightaway using legal aid, and he was released on bail and reunited with his heartbroken wife and children again. The God sent Solicitor made a family application to the Home office on the basis of a fourteen years long stay, children over seven years, and compassionate grounds, and they were speedily granted their indefinite stay within three months. Praise God! The Bible says in ***Romans 8:28***,

> 28 *"And we know that all things work together for good to them that love God, to them who are the called according to his purpose."*

What is it you are going through today? I encourage you to be positive, and optimistic that God is working behind the scenes to make all things work together for your good in Jesus' name. Amen!

CHAPTER SEVENTY-SEVEN

THE STORMS OF LIFE – POEM

No one is immune to the storms of life
Old, Young, Righteous, Unrighteous, absolutely no one!
The storms came raging at me
And I was caught in the fierce hurricane
And while the monster whirlwind enveloped me
I put my full trust in Christ Jesus,
Knowing that He will never leave me nor forsake me
I remained calm like one gliding on surf in the ocean
Knowing that Jesus is with me all the way
Jesus saved me.
I opened my eyes and realised
I have been in a dream. Whao!

I was caught up again in another storm
This time an even more deadly storm
This time a reality, not a dream
I immediately remained calm,
Knowing that Jesus is with me all the way
While the monster whirlwind enveloped me
And flew me at an amazing speed
And miraculously I came to rest unhurt,
And that's because I did not doubt when I saw the boisterous wind.
I trusted Jesus,
And He saved me.
Rest in Christ as you go through the storms of life
And it will pass like a dream.

CHAPTER SEVENTY-EIGHT

DON'T ENVY FRAUDSTERS

Some people are so heartless and all they do for a living is swindling, cheating, stealing, and defrauding innocent people of their valuables. As they carry out their wicked acts, they even see it as fun. I had to include this message in this book in order to get readers to be on guard against being a victim of fraud which in turn could leave the victim in emotional pain needing healing. Prevention is better than cure. Thank God the Bible has also made clear the consequences of fraud, and the Most High God Himself will see to it.

Don't envy fraudsters for anything because they are living a false life. They only ***seem*** to be prospering. It's just going to be a question of time, and they will be caught by the Police, tried in court, and sentenced to prison, and their loot will dwindle away mysteriously over time. And if the state does not catch and penalise them, God will judge them and they will likely end up in hell fire. There is no hiding place for fraudsters. Let's look at a passage from the Bible below about fraudsters. ***Psalm 73:3-8 &12,***

> *3For I was envious at the foolish, when I saw the prosperity of the wicked.*
>
> *4For there are no bands in their death: but their strength is firm.*
>
> *5They are not in trouble as other men; neither are they plagued like other men.*
>
> *6Therefore pride compasseth them about as a chain; violence covereth them as a garment.*
>
> *7Their eyes stand out with fatness: they have more than heart could wish.*

[8]They are corrupt, and speak wickedly concerning oppression: they speak loftily...

[12]Behold, these are the ungodly, who prosper in the world; they increase in riches.

We don't need to envy fraudsters for anything. King David wrote in ***Psalm 37:1-2*** saying,

[1]Fret not thyself because of evildoers, neither be thou envious against the workers of iniquity.

[2]For they shall soon be cut down like the grass, and wither as the green herb.

WHAT THE BIBLE SAYS ABOUT FRAUD.

1. The Bible says in ***Exodus 20:15***, *"Thou shalt not steal."* The Bible has clearly stated here that stealing is not good. Therefore, it is certain there is penalty for disobedience, except for where the mercy of God prevails.
2. The Bible says again in ***Jeremiah 17:11***, *"As the partridge sitteth on eggs, and hatcheth them not; so he that getteth riches, and not by right, shall leave them in the midst of his days, and at his end shall be a fool."* When something is written in the Bible, consider it as authentic and certain to happen. The riches gotten by fraudsters are not by right. Therefore, in line with this scripture, they are certainly going to leave all the stolen money in the midst of their days and end up as a fool in life. That's what this scripture says. They may be smiling now, but somehow, the Word of God has a way of coming to pass.
3. The Bible says again in ***Proverbs 13:11***, *"Wealth gotten by vanity shall be diminished: but he that gathereth by labour shall increase."* (NIV) puts it this way, *"Dishonest money dwindles away,..."* And Amplified Bible says, wealth gotten ***unjustly*** will dwindle away. This scripture guarantees the fact that all the loot fraudsters get will certainly diminish or dwindle away. It's just a question of time, and it will happen.

4. ***Proverbs 23:5*** says, "*Wilt thou set thine eyes upon that which is not? for riches certainly make themselves wings; they fly away as an eagle toward heaven.*" It's better to trust God, and not in fraudulent riches because such riches have a tendency of making themselves wings, and flying away. The loot of fraudsters is temporary because all the money they steal is sure to mysteriously disappear and fly away as an eagle toward heaven. That's what this verse says, and it is authentic.
5. ***Galatians 6:7*** says, *Be not deceived; God is not mocked: for whatsoever a man soweth, that shall he also reap.* "This scripture says, if somebody sows fraud, he will also reap fraud. When you defraud somebody, somebody else will also defraud you. Jacob swindled Esau of his blessing and fled to his uncle Laban in Padanaram. When he got there, his uncle also defrauded him by making him labour for Rachel 14 years instead of 7 years, and also changed his wages ten times and would have even hurt him. Read what Jacob said in ***Genesis 31:7***, "*And your father hath deceived me, and changed my wages ten times; but God suffered him not to hurt me.*" What goes round comes round.
6. Finally, ***Isaiah 57:21*** says, "*There is no peace, saith my God, to the wicked.*" It's wickedness for fraudsters to cause their victims to be in pain and sorrow. Therefore, they can't have peace. Anyone committing fraud must know that they can't escape the Judgment of God.

CHAPTER SEVENTY-NINE

JOB INTERVIEW TIPS

Once again, somebody may be reading this book and ask, "What has job interview tips got to do with healing?" The truth is that periods of unemployment are usually challenging times, and knowing the right interview tips will get you the right job, which in turn can help bring forth healing through financial provisions, increased comfort, confidence, and self-esteem. As you prepare to attend a job interview, here are a few tips you may find very useful.

1. Pray that you will be preferred and chosen.
2. Pray that the interview panel will only ask you for what you have, and not ask you for what you don't have. For example, pray that they don't ask you for qualifications or experience which you don't have.
3. Uphold integrity by telling them the truth regarding any question they ask you believing that God will back your integrity. Avoid falsifying anything.
4. Read your job description, person specification, and your application form properly because you are basically facing the panel to defend what you wrote on the application form or on your CV.
5. Read leaflets, or go on the internet and read general background information about the company or organisation you want to work for.
6. Ensure you get to the interview venue at least 20 minutes before the scheduled time. Don't be late.
7. Ensure your dressing is formal, and your hair nicely done. Avoid lots of make-up. It's better to be modest.
8. It may be a good idea to find someone who is doing a similar job who you can interact with and perhaps rehearse your

application form with. Note their suggestions, criticisms, and corrections.

9. Have ready answers to questions like:

   What background information do you know about this Company?
   Why do you think we should hire you?
   What are your expectations in the next five years?
   What is equal opportunity policy?

10. Relax yourself at the interview. Although it's an interview, come with the mentality that you will be yourself and flow with the panel naturally. Be bold, and humorous when need be.
11. Remember to come with your portfolio – certificates, awards, testimonials, writing materials etc.
12. While the interview is on, ensure you present and sell yourself well without lying on anything. The truth you say is more likely to give you the job than lies as a Christian.
13. If they say, any questions? Ask questions like:

    Do you have training and development programme for employees in order for them to improve themselves, as well as have promotion prospects?
    Ask them about general welfare benefits and incentives for employees.
    Let them know you are a Christian and you will like to be in church on Sundays. This is important for a job that requires employees to work weekends.

14. Ask the panel to repeat any question that is not clear to you so that you will give the right answer. Don't assume you understand the question. And give clear and concise answers using relevant professional terms.
15. While the interview is going on, ensure you sit upright and have good eye contact.
16. Before, and during the interview, put up a cheerful appearance. Give a warm firm handshake before and after the interview.
17. Finally, continually expect, and picture it in your mind that the job is yours. See yourself as the chosen person and it shall be so in Jesus' name. Amen!

CHAPTER EIGHTY

IT IS WELL – 2 KINGS 4

What do you say when you face the pressures of life? What do you say when you are squeezed, and crushed by acute trails? Do you lose control so much that you swear and say negative things, complain and blame people and things? The way you react to challenging situations and circumstances truly reflects who you are. A calm and positive attitude demonstrates a godly nature and is more likely to secure victory.

Two men were on an airplane flight and serious turbulence commenced in the air. Mr A broke down in tears crying and saying, "I'm dead today. So this is how my life will just end today." And Mr B started confessing scriptures confidently saying, "It is well with me, the entire persons on board, and this flight. We shall not die but live to declare the works of God. No weapon of turbulence formed against us shall prosper. We shall surely land safely in Jesus' name. Amen!"

From the words spoken by the two men you can see that Mr A is cowardly, worldly and devoid of the Word of God, while Mr B is confident, godly, and saturated with the Word of God. I believe you will prefer to be close to Mr B to boost your confidence rather than Mr A who will dampen the spirit of those around him.

In *2 Kings 4:18–37* we see the story of the Shunamite woman. She lost her only precious child, yet she still had the grace and calm to say, "It is well." After the child died, she said to the husband in verse 23 "*...It shall be well*". Prophet Elisha asked his servant Gehazi to meet her and ask her about her family, she said, ***"It is well." 2 Kings 4:26*** says, "*Run now, I pray thee, to meet her, and say unto her, Is it well with thee? is it well with thy husband? is it well with the child? And she answered, It is well:*"

What can be more devastating than for a woman to lose her only son? And amidst that she still had the courage to say, "It is well." It's important to note two things here. First, she was saying it is well by faith believing that it will turn out to be well as she says it. Secondly, it truly turned out to be well as she continued to say it is well as her son was restored back to life by Prophet Elisha in verse 35. What we say when we are passing through trials, as well as our attitude can either prolong the trials or end it speedily. The reason why we have to say positive things and also put up positive attitude is because ***Proverbs 18:21*** says, "*Death and life are in the power of the tongue...*" To silence the enemy during trials, constantly sing the chorus of the hymn, "***It is well with my soul.***"

CHAPTER EIGHTY-ONE

FAITHFULNESS

God is still very much in the business of blessing Christians even on a daily basis. How do I know this? I know this because the scriptures made it clear in ***Psalm 68:19*** that "*...He daily loadeth us with benefits...*" But there is one thing that is coming against this promise of God to reward us with blessings daily, and that is unfaithfulness. In a nutshell, faithfulness means to trust, believe, and be loyal. It also means to keep one's promise; be accurate, and precise in carrying out one's duty.

The Christian walk for many, especially babes in Christ, has become a case of one step forward, two steps backwards. It has become a case of if God doesn't grant my request, I will quit. My friend, you don't need to do that. Have a personal assessment of yourself and ask, "What is my motivation of serving God? I'm I serving God faithfully?" Do a honest soul searching. Are you serving God because you love Him and sincerely worship Him in spirit and in truth? Do you see God as "A Heavenly Fixer?" Do you see God as one whose ***main*** duty is to sort out your problems and supply your needs? Mind you, God also has expectations. For example, God expects your praise and worship, and thanksgiving. He also needs you to win souls. The reason why this message is coming to you today is because God wants you to examine yourself properly in the area of faithfulness.

The Bible says in ***Proverbs 28:20***, "*A faithful man shall abound with blessings: but he that maketh haste to be rich shall not be innocent.*" The **'A'** part of this scripture is for faithful people, while the **'B'** part of this scripture is for unfaithful people. Unfaithful people want God to load them daily with benefits, but they are not ready to pay the price. They think they are smart, and as such they are in a haste to be rich, even while being unfaithful. Unfortunately, the things of God are not that way.

God wants us to examine ourselves in every area of our Christian life and wake up to the call of faithfulness. God wants you to be faithful with your tithing, church attendance, church work, punctual to church, your secular job, and business. He wants you to be faithful with your prayers, praise and worship, just to mention a few. As you do this, you will surely abound with blessings in due season. I can see God honouring your faithfulness. So, don't give up! Don't faint! Don't backslide! Just hang in there and hold on to Jesus. Remember ***Revelation 2:10*** says, "*...Be thou faithful unto death, and I will give thee a crown of life.*" God bless you abundantly as you remain faithful in every area of your Christian walk.

CHAPTER EIGHTY-TWO

DO YOU REALLY BELIEVE?

When you fully trust the Word of God, it truly helps to put a person at rest no matter the bombardments from the enemy, situations, and circumstances. God is not man that He should lie concerning the things He has promised or spoken about you. Simply remain focused on God and don't doubt His word, and He will surely bring it to pass at the appointed time.

Isaiah 28:16

> *"Therefore thus saith the Lord God, Behold, I lay in Zion for a foundation a stone, a tried stone, a precious corner stone, a sure foundation: he that believeth shall not make haste."*

To believe in God means to trust, rely, and have faith and confidence in the Lord that He will do that which you believe. It also means that even if you have not seen the manifestation of what you believe God for, you know it fully well that it will surely come to pass. Unbelievers want to see to believe. But for born again Christians, you have to fully believe, to see the manifestation.

If you truly believe:

You will not be in a hurry.
You will not worry.
You will not panic.
You will not be troubled.
You will not fret.
You will be patient.
You will be calm.
You will be still.

Psalms 46:10

> *"Be still, and know that I am God: I will be exalted among the heathen, I will be exalted in the earth."*

I know of a man whose character is worthy of emulation in the Bible. His name is Job. The man believes God fully therefore he is ready to wait all the days of his life till his change comes. Job doesn't care about the circumstances around him. His mind is made up to wait on God to grant his requests at the appointed time. Read what he said in ***Job 14:14***, *"If a man die, shall he live again? all the days of my appointed time will I wait, till my change come."*

You don't fully believe if you get into mood swings, and it reflects externally because you carry about a long face so that people now ask you, "Are you ok?" My friend, cheer up! Jesus has already overcome the world. You are an overcomer. You are more than a conqueror. He that believeth shall not make haste. Don't be in a hurry. Be patient. The Lord is working it out behind the scenes. Receive the manifestation by faith in Jesus' name. Amen!

CHAPTER EIGHTY-THREE

THE MIRACLE MEAL – HOLY COMMUNION

The Holy Communion is a blessed miracle meal made up of two elements, the bread, and non-alcoholic wine. These two elements represent the body and blood of Jesus Christ of Nazareth. And we are to take it by faith in remembrance of the Lord. Many people I know have shared testimonies how they took the communion and they received their healing. This confirms that the communion is a powerful element for healing provided you take it by faith.

1 Corinthians 11:24

> *"And when he had given thanks, he brake it, and said, Take, eat: this is my body, which is broken for you: this do in remembrance of me."*

The Holy Communion, after it has been blessed, is infused with the Zoe power of God, and when taken by faith, has the capacity to produce any kind of miracle in a person's life, and that includes believers and unbelievers.

BENEFITS OF TAKING HOLY COMMUNION

1. ETERNAL LIFE

John 6:53–54

> 53*Then Jesus said unto them, Verily, verily, I say unto you, Except ye eat the flesh of the Son of man, and drink his blood, ye have no life in you.*

[54]Whoso eateth my flesh, and drinketh my blood, hath eternal life; and I will raise him up at the last day.

2. BRINGS HEALING, STOPS MISCARRIAGE, AND BARRENNESS

Exodus 23:25–26

[25]And ye shall serve the Lord your God, and he shall bless thy bread, and thy water; and I will take sickness away from the midst of thee.

[26]There shall nothing cast their young, nor be barren, in thy land: the number of thy days I will fulfil.

3. OPENS OUR SPIRITUAL EYES, GLADENS AND STRENGTHENS THE HEART

Luke 24:30–31

[30]And it came to pass, as he sat at meat with them, he took bread, and blessed it, and brake, and gave to them.

[31]And their eyes were opened, and they knew him; and he vanished out of their sight.

Psalms 104:15

"And wine that maketh glad the heart of man, and oil to make his face to shine, and bread which strengtheneth man's heart."

4. REMISSION OF SINS

Matthew 26:26–28

[26]And as they were eating, Jesus took bread, and blessed it, and brake it, and gave it to the disciples, and said, Take, eat; this is my body.

> [27]*And he took the cup, and gave thanks, and gave it to them, saying, Drink ye all of it;*
>
> [28]*For this is my blood of the new testament, which is shed for many for the remission of sins.*

5. BLESSINGS

1 Corinthians 10:16

> *"The cup of blessing which we bless, is it not the communion of the blood of Christ? The bread which we break, is it not the communion of the body of Christ?"*

You must take the Holy Communion reverentially by faith. I have seen and heard testimonies of how the communion brought forth healings and deliverances. For example, a woman shared her testimony with me saying she had fibroids and it was Holy Communion she had in church and fibroids died forever. Hallelujah! So, take the Holy Communion with expectations that something miraculous will happen in your life.

CHAPTER EIGHTY-FOUR

KEEP YOUR OWN WORDS – THAT'S INTEGRITY!

This message is very important because when you keep your own words it helps to make you be at peace. The person you made a promise to will not trouble you for not keeping your word. And to be at peace with men brings forth healing. Keeping your own word also brings you a sense of fulfillment and joy. Besides, keeping your own word is a mark of integrity.

Matthew12:36-37

> [36]*But I say unto you, That every idle word that men shall speak, they shall give account thereof in the day of judgment.*
>
> [37]*For by thy words thou shalt be justified, and by thy words thou shalt be condemned.*

The above scripture makes it clear that we will give account of every idle or careless word we speak in the day of judgment. Tough! This is certainly calling us to order to avoid speaking recklessly, and think before we speak. We ought to weigh our words before we speak and ensure what we say is right, and that we make good our promises. The Most High God is a God of integrity. He is forever committed and faithful to keep His Word. We ought to exhibit this quality as children of God created in His own image. Let your yea be yea, and nay be nay!

CONSEQUENCES OF NOT KEEPING YOUR OWN WORDS

1. When you say things and you don't do it, you automatically appear to be or become a liar. And Revelation 21:8 says all liars will end up in hell.
2. People lose confidence and trust in you if you don't keep to your words.
3. You can lose friends and customers because you don't keep to your words.
4. Remember you will give account of every idle careless word you speak which you don't keep to in the day of judgment. Read Matthew 12:36 above again.
5. Remember you will be justified or condemned by your own words in the day of judgment. Read Matthew 12:37 above again.
6. You create a bad impression for yourself when you don't keep to your own words.

ADVICE

1. Always think before you speak. Evaluate what you want to say whether you will be able to do it or not.
2. Do not promise what you can't fulfil. It is more honourable to remain silent than to promise what you can't deliver.
3. Be humble enough to apologise when you fail to do what you promised.

We are created in the image of God. Therefore, imitate God by saying what you mean, and mean what you say. God bless you in Jesus' name. Amen!!

CHAPTER EIGHTY-FIVE

DESTINED TO SOAR

According to the *Merriam Webster Dictionary*, destiny means, "A predetermined course of events often held to be an irresistible power or agency; a power that is believed to control what happens in the future." To soar means, "To fly or sail often at a great height by floating on air currents; to rise up quickly to a great height; to ascend to higher or more exalted level; to rise to majestic stature."

When we talk of soaring, one animal that immediately comes to mind is the eagle. The eagle is a unique bird with great strength and power, and very sharp focus to watch and notice things from a far distance. One interesting thing about the eagle is that it does not start soaring right from birth. It goes through a process or transformation before it starts soaring. From egg to eaglet, juvenile eagle, and then to a full grown eagle that soars. Similarly, human beings also have to go through a process before they can start soaring. However, this process is beyond physical maturity. The Bible says in Luke 2:52 that Jesus increased in wisdom and stature and was in favour with God and man. To soar, there has to be increase in wisdom and stature.

IMPORTANT THINGS TO NOTE ABOUT BEING DESTINED TO SOAR

We must be ***conscious*** of the fact that we are destined to soar. The Bible tells us clearly that we are created in God's own image. This effectively means that we have similar characteristics as our Creator. God is supernatural and extraordinary in His ways. And those who are destined to soar are conscious of the fact that they are created in God's own image to operate in the supernatural, and manifesting extraordinary things just like God. Those who are not conscious of this fact may never soar.

Genesis 1:27–28

> [27]*So God created man in his own image, in the image of God created he him; male and female created he them.*
>
> [28]*And God blessed them, and God said unto them, Be fruitful, and multiply, and replenish the earth, and subdue it: and have dominion over the fish of the sea, and over the fowl of the air, and over every living thing that moveth upon the earth.*

Verse 28 above also makes it clear that after man was created, God blessed them, saying be fruitful, and multiply and replenish the earth, and subdue it: and have dominion over things. This statement by God suggests that God's original plan and destiny for man is for him to soar.

The Bible says we are fearfully and wonderfully made. This also suggests that God created us and predestined us to do great things including to soar. Those who are fearfully and wonderfully made do exploits, and attain great heights in achievements.

Psalms 139:14

> *"I will praise thee; for I am fearfully and wonderfully made: marvellous are thy works; and that my soul knoweth right well."*

THINGS TO DO TO START MANIFESTING A SOARING LIFESTYLE

It is good to know and be conscious of the fact that we are destined to soar. However, it is another thing to begin to manifest this soaring lifestyle. It takes a work and a process to start manifesting it. If you don't do anything, you are likely not to soar in life. Let's look at a few things one needs to do to soar.

1. BE BORN AGAIN AND BE FILLED WITH THE HOLY GHOST

To soar in life requires going through a process just like the eagle. And the starting point should be to become a born again Christian, and then be filled with the Holy Spirit. This is very important because Christians can only truly soar when they are empowered by the Holy Ghost.

2 Corinthians 5:17

> *"Therefore if any man be in Christ, he is a new creature: old things are passed away; behold, all things are become new."*

When you give your life to Jesus, you become a new creature with recreated spirit filled with the Holy Ghost and this empowers you to soar in life.

Does this now mean those who are not born again Christians cannot soar in life? Good question! They can because we have seen people who believe in other religions and even so called atheists who have achieved great things in life. Essentially, they were able to achieve greatness by ***'faith'*** in whatever they believe. However, for the purpose of this message, we will be focusing on Christians.

2. PREPARE TO SOAR

Nothing great just happens in life. It takes preparation, careful planning, and effort to get off from a state of inertia to moving slowly, and to running, and then flying and soaring.

2 Chronicles 27:6

> *"So Jotham became mighty, because he prepared his ways before the Lord his God."*

For Jotham to become mighty, he had to prepare for it, and he did that from God's perspective. He didn't become mighty by accident or by being lucky. One essential thing we need in order to excel in life is quality education and training. This will go a long way to enhance our skills and ability regarding whatever we are out to achieve. Training definitely helps us master our plans.

Even the eagle mother trains the eaglet on how to fly. Part of the training has to do with making the nest uncomfortable for the eaglet, and carrying it on the back to fly. You must leave your comfort zone and be ready to work in order to soar.

3. HAVE A VISION

Those who soar in life do have a clear vision about their purpose in life. They don't live their life aimlessly. When you have a godly vision, God makes a provision. You must have a dream or goals as a target that you have set your eyes to achieve. And the goal must be big, and capable of driving you to achieve.

Proverbs 29:18

> *"Where there is no vision, the people perish: but he that keepeth the law, happy is he."*

Habakkuk 2:2–4 – Write your vision down and continually review it.

Those who truly soar in life are focused, not allowing anything to distract them. Just the way the eagle focuses on its prey, that's how they focus on their goals, targeting it with precision and then scoring goals.

4. WALK WITH THE WISE

Those who truly soar in life are mindful of their associations. To soar means you have to surround yourself with wise people who have achieved great things and who will help you achieve greatness. Have a ***mentor*** who will coach you on the right path to follow to achieve greatness. Avoid small minded people who are likely to bring you down to their own level. The Bible says in,

Proverbs 13:20

> *"He that walketh with wise men shall be wise: but a companion of fools shall be destroyed."*

Eagles fly and soar alone at very high altitudes. They have no business associating themselves with pigeons, sparrows, or doves flying at very low levels. Fly with other eagles and soar achieving great things.

5. THE STORMS OF LIFE

Eagles love the storm. When the clouds gather, the eagle gets excited because it uses the storm's wind to lift itself higher. Once the eagle finds the wind of the storm, it uses the raging storm to lift itself above the clouds. This gives the eagle an opportunity to glide and rest its wings. Meanwhile, all the other birds go into hiding because of the storm.

Those who soar in life face their challenges head on, knowing that the challenges will make them emerge stronger and better. We can use the storms of life to rise to greater heights. Achievers are not afraid to rise to greater heights. Achievers are not afraid of challenges; rather they relish them and use them profitably.

Great achievers connect to the supernatural power of God through prayers, praises, Bible study, and the power of the Holy Ghost to overcome the storms of life.

2 Corinthians 4:16–17

> 16*For which cause we faint not; but though our outward man perish, yet the inward man is renewed day by day.*
>
> 17*For our light affliction, which is but for a moment, worketh for us a far more exceeding and eternal weight of glory;*

6. BE DILIGENT

To soar in life requires a lot of diligence. Therefore, hard work is a necessary ingredient for anyone who truly desires to soar in life.

Proverbs 22:29

> *"Seest thou a man diligent in his business? he shall stand before kings; he shall not stand before mean men."*

7. SACRIFICE

Going through the Bible, we can see that one of the things people did to achieve greatness and to soar was to give quality offerings and sacrifice. King Solomon, known to be the wisest and wealthiest king that ever lived achieved that status through giving. He prospered immensely. King Solomon's offering attracted God's attention.

1 Kings 3:3–4

> 3*And Solomon loved the Lord, walking in the statutes of David his father: only he sacrificed and burnt incense in high places.*
>
> 4*And the king went to Gibeon to sacrifice there; for that was the great high place: a thousand burnt offerings did Solomon offer upon that altar.*

One of the best ways to soar in life is to follow the footsteps of those who have soared. Do what they did. Understudy them by reading autobiographies and biographies. Solomon sacrificed. Do the same thing.

8. SHED AWAY BAD HABITS AND AVOID SIN

When the eagle starts growing old at about 40 years, its feathers becomes weak and cannot take it as fast and as high as it should. This makes the eagle weak and could lead to death. So, the eagle retires to a place far away in the mountains, and begins to pluck out the weak feathers on its body; and break its beaks and claws against the rocks until it is completely bare. This is a very bloody and painful process which lasts for about 150 days. Then the eagle stays in this hiding place until it grows new feathers, new beaks, and claws and then comes out flying higher than before, and living for another 30 years making it a total of about 70 years all together.

Similarly, those who desire to soar in life must get rid of bad habits that are capable of hindering progress and prosperity. They are weights that must be given up in order to move up in life light. There should be a season of fasting, reflection, and quiet time with God. A season when you shut down your mobile phone, internet, social media and other forms of distractions and meaningfully engage in spiritual exercise in prayer, Bible study, praises etc.

The Bible says the wages of sin is death. Sin leads to spiritual death; hence it has to be avoided like plague in order to soar in life. In a nutshell, those who desire to soar in life must choose to live upright and honest life.

9. GOOD SUCCESS

In one verse, the Bible makes it clear what we should do in order to have good success. Any Christian who truly desires to soar should pay attention to this formula in this verse and apply it in their life.

Joshua 1:8

> *"This book of the law shall not depart out of thy mouth; but thou shalt meditate therein day and night, that thou mayest observe to do according to all that is written therein: for then thou shalt make thy way prosperous, and then thou shalt have good success."*

10. GATHER MOMENTUM

Looking at how the airplane takes off and then goes on to soar will give us a good picture of how to soar in life. The airplane first takes off by moving slowly and then starts speeding up gathering more and more momentum as it takes off, rising so high into the cloud until it gets to the right altitude where it begins to cruise effortlessly expending very little power as it glides like an eagle.

Similarly, for anyone to soar in life, they have to plan it carefully and take off gathering momentum as they take off with great speed until they start flying and cruising effortlessly at very high altitude through the power of the Holy Spirit. Gathering momentum is about building up yourself immensely through increase in knowledge and spiritual exercise while connecting and depending on the Holy Spirit.

Isaiah 40:31

> *"But they that wait upon the Lord shall renew their strength; they shall mount up with wings as eagles; they shall run, and not be weary; and they shall walk, and not faint."*

You are destined to soar! Get off from the ground level by faith and mount up with wings as an eagle and begin to soar in the name of Jesus. Amen!

CHAPTER EIGHTY-SIX

EVANGELISE!

To win lost souls into the kingdom of God is a mandate for every believer. Jesus commanded all Christians, including you to evangelise. He says in

Mark 16:15

> *"And he said unto them, Go ye into all the world, and preach the gospel to every creature."*

Matthew 28:19–20

> [19]*Go ye therefore, and teach all nations, baptising them in the name of the Father, and of the Son, and of the Holy Ghost:*
>
> [20]*Teaching them to observe all things whatsoever I have commanded you: and, lo, I am with you alway, even unto the end of the world. Amen.*

According to the scriptures below, soul winners are wise and stars forever. Therefore, use every available opportunity to evangelise and win souls. Read what the Bible says below.

Proverbs 11:30

> *"The fruit of the righteous is a tree of life; and he that winneth souls is wise."*

Daniel 12:3

> *"And they that be wise shall shine as the brightness of the firmament; and they that turn many to righteousness as the stars for ever and ever."*

There are souls to be won everywhere. Influence unbelievers positively and draw them to receive salvation.

YOUR GOOD CHARACTER towards unbelievers is one of the most effective ways of winning souls. Therefore, as a Christian, determine to be upright in your ways, and promote the gospel everywhere. Remember, unbelievers are watching your behaviour even without you knowing it. They are watching to see if you are living out your life as a God fearing Christian. Action they say, speaks louder than words. Once they are convinced about your good character, they will be very willing to accept Jesus as their Lord and Saviour. But if you exhibit bad character before them, they may not even listen to you to accept Jesus. Don't be ashamed to declare you are a Christian and preach to win souls. Be confident and bold as you meet people.

Romans 1:16

> *"For I am not ashamed of the gospel of Christ: for it is the power of God unto salvation to everyone that believeth; to the Jew first, and also to the Greek."*

The harvest is truly plentiful, but the labourers are few. Be one of the reapers, because the labourer is worthy of his wages. See John 4:34–38 of The Living Bible. Jesus is lord everywhere. Therefore, there is absolutely no place you cannot win souls provided the people are ready to listen to you.

SPREAD THE GOOD NEWS

Welldone! You have successfully finished reading this book. I believe you must have picked up some principles that will help you grow in the Word of God, and spiritually as you apply them in your life. It is the application of the principles you have learnt that will bring about a transformation in your life and also give you your desired results. So, keep on practicing what you have learnt.

Now that you have read this book, and you are blessed, I would like you to tell your family, friends, and colleagues about this book. Spread the good news of the principles you have learnt. Recommend this book to at least twenty people you know. You can even get some copies for your loved ones as a gift. As you do this, you become a blessing to others and also enlighten the world from where you are. Thank you and God bless you abundantly.

MICHAEL NWADUBA

BIBLIOGRAPHY

1. The Holy Bible containing the Old and New Testaments. Authorized King James Version. Reference Edition. Thomas Nelson Bibles, A Division of Thomas Nelson, Inc. Copyright 1989 Thomas Nelson Inc. Printed in the United States of America.
2. The Living Bible. Parents Resource Bible. A Life Application Bible. Edysyl Publications. Parents Resource Bible. Copyright 1995 by Tyndale House Publishers.
3. The Amplified Bible. Copyright 1954, 1958, 1962, 1964, 1965, 1987 by The Lockman Foundation.
4. The Thompson Chain-Reference Study Bible. Second Improved Edition. New International Version. Copyright 1973, 1978, 1984 by International Bible Society.
5. Matt Morris: Chinese bamboo -http://www.mattmorris.com/how-success-is-like-a-chinese-bamboo-tree/–(Accessed October 5, 2017)
6. John Assaraf: How to set and achieve goals' video –http://www.bing.com/search?q=Internet+video– +How+to+set+and+achieve+any+goal+you+have+in+your+life+by+John+Assaraf&src=IE-TopResult&FORM=IETR02&conversationid=&adlt=strict - (Accessed October 5, 2017)

All scriptural references in this book are taken from the King James Version except where indicated.

FOR INFORMATION, ENQUIRIES, OR BOOKINGS TO SPEAK:

Please send all correspondence directly to:
Email: mikenwaduba@gmail.com

OTHER BOOKS WRITTEN BY THE AUTHOR

1. A Simple Guide for Bible Study
2. Questions and Answers on Tithes: Covenant of Prosperity
3. Amazing Grace in Abundance
4. Mr and Mrs Evans' Honeymoon on the Island of Majorca, Spain

To order the above books log into: ***www.Amazon.co.uk***

ABOUT THE AUTHOR

Michael Nwaduba is a Minister of God with a calling to write and evangelise. Prior to God's calling into ministry, he obtained qualifications in Business Administration, and Accountancy. He worked for nearly two decades as a finance officer for various establishments including being a Church Administrator for a Pentecostal Church in London.

He teaches the truth in the Word of God with a passion. He firmly believes in the integrity of the Word of God. You will find his books interesting and easy to understand because of the simple style he adopts as an author. You will also find biblical and practical life examples in his books.

Minister Mike is also a lawyer. He obtained his LLB (Hons) Law degree from London South Bank University, London, United Kingdom. He is a member of RCCG Victory House, London, and also the Personal Assistant (PA) to Pastor Leke Sanusi, Special Assistant to The General Overseer (SATGO), RCCG Europe Mainland Region 2.

www.ingramcontent.com/pod-product-compliance
Lightning Source LLC
LaVergne TN
LVHW011346080426
835511LV00005B/155

* 9 7 8 1 7 8 6 2 3 4 6 9 8 *